LANGUAGE STRATEGIES FOR LITTLE ONES

Michele Fagan, M.S., CCC-SLP

Vicki Prouty, M.S., CCC-SLP

Super Duper® Publications
Greenville, South Carolina

11 10 09 08 07 06 11 10 9 8 7 6 5 4

Library of Congress Cataloging-in-Publication Data

Fagan, Michele, date

Language strategies for little ones / Michele Fagan, Vicki Prouty.

p. cm.

Includes bibliographical references.

ISBN 978-1-888222-30-2 (pbk.)

1. Speech therapy for children—Exercises. 2. Learning disabled children—Education (Primary)—Problems, exercises, etc. 3. Language arts (Primary)—Problems, exercises, etc. 4. Children-Language—Problems, exercises, etc. 5. Language experience approach in education—Problems, exercises, etc. I. Prouty, Vicki L. II. Title.

LB3454.F35 1998

371.91'4—dc21 98-35119

CIP

Printed in USA

Illustrations by Patti Argoff

P. O. Box 24997 • Greenville, SC 29616-2497 USA
www.superduperinc.com
1-800-277-8738 • FAX: 1-800-978-7379

DEDICATION

To our husbands and families,
who have continued to provide their support and enthusiasm
through all of our writing endeavors

TABLE OF CONTENTS

PREFACE

Language Strategies for Little Ones was developed to provide a simplified version of the book *Language Strategies for Children* that would be appropriate for a primary-age population. We wanted a program that would provide a flow of skills starting at the kindergarten level and continuing through the upper elementary grades. Now, with the addition of *Language Strategies for Little Ones,* the educator can teach these important language strategies at a developmentally appropriate level. Our younger students have benefited from the social application stories, which helped them recognize the value of learning skills such as using question words to gather information and recognizing story grammar elements. And the Einstein character has made learning and practicing fun for young children.

We have enjoyed developing this comprehensive program that has been a benefit both for children and for parents. We hope that educators and speech-language pathologists will find that the use of this resource will make them more effective and confident in meeting the needs of their students.

Special thanks to the supportive administrators, teachers, parents, and students at Wells and Saigling Elementary Schools of Plano, Texas. We wish to specifically thank the second-grade and kindergarten teachers for their input and collaboration and for allowing us to spend time in their classrooms. We also want to thank our reviewers—Peg Hutson-Nechkash, Robin Kanis, and Linda Roth—who helped to shape this resource.

INTRODUCTION

OVERVIEW

Since 1990, the inclusion movement has prompted a shift in focus for providing special services to children with exceptional needs. In considering the "least restrictive environment" provision of the Individuals with Disabilities Education Act (IDEA), educators are part of a movement to provide services within the classroom setting when appropriate. Naremore (1995) terms this service delivery as *classroom-based intervention*. The speech-language pathologist or learning disabilities specialist provides services in the classroom, sometimes teaching alongside the classroom teacher and sometimes building around or supplementing the lessons being taught in the classroom (Naremore, 1995). It is as important as ever to ensure that students are successful in the classroom setting. Students need strategies for success. The strategies presented in *Language Strategies for Little Ones* are appropriate for classroom-based intervention.

Language Strategies for Little Ones is a multifaceted tool for developing the communication skills of students in kindergarten and first grade. The lessons integrate whole language philosophy, classroom curriculum concepts, literature-based intervention techniques, and strategies for self-prompting. This resource capitalizes on students' visual strengths by providing creative, visual reminders of strategies. Memorable strategy names help students internalize their use. Use of the strategies in other settings is encouraged through homework assignments and vacation calendar activities. The program components include lessons, homework activities, skills checklists, parent newsletters, and a summer calendar. These materials work together to maximize learning, generalization, and skill maintenance.

Language Strategies for Little Ones embeds Hunter's (1982) lesson cycle format and the principles of brain-based research discussed by Caine and Caine (1991) and Kavalic and Olsen (1993). It provides activities that will appeal to students with different learning styles, so each child has an opportunity for success in learning about communication. As a way to reach students with learning problems, Rief (1993) proposes the use of multisensory methods to promote interest, relevancy, and motivation. In addition, these methods stress active participation and interaction among peers. Multisensory methods are applied throughout the *Language Strategies for Little Ones* lessons.

Communication goals focus on three primary areas: (1) language comprehension, (2) oral expression, and (3) story grammar knowledge, which to enhance remembrance will be called simply "story knowledge" in the lessons. An organizational chart (see page 15) cross-references individual lessons to lesson objectives. Engaging literature is integral to teaching the goals and objectives. Creative links to curriculum are made through a variety of materials (e.g., various art prints by the masters are used to practice listening skills; compare time periods; and learn about seasons, climates, and land regions). *Language Strategies for Little Ones* is an ideal tool for schools implementing an inclusion model. Activities are interactive and include reading, writing, role-playing, and art. Suggestions for adapting lessons for small group settings and suggestions for varying lessons are included.

Program Goals

Four main goals are emphasized in *Language Strategies for Little Ones*:

1. To provide students with multisensory strategies that
   - promote self-learning and self-prompting
   - decrease the need for direct assistance from an adult
   - help them experience success in the least restrictive classroom environment possible
2. To teach in a way that integrates curriculum concepts by
   - using materials that tie in to a primary curriculum
   - planning activities that complement development of skills for school success
3. To introduce an awareness of student responsibility for learning by
   - providing social application stories that concretely represent the importance of the lesson at a primary level
   - providing a visual framework for awareness of strategy components
4. To develop a system that encourages parent participation by
   - increasing their awareness of the children's program and goals
   - providing quick, easy, home-related activities that pertain to language goals

Intended Users

Language Strategies for Little Ones can be used in small group settings and in large group or classroom settings. Educators who strive for students to become independent learners and generalizers of skills in the classroom, at home, and, eventually, in work environments will find this resource useful. Strategies for learning are appropriate for all students, though the primary focus of this resource is students with learning difficulties. The lessons are appropriate for students in kindergarten and first grade, or those who are functioning at that level developmentally. Although most activities are written for group participation, the lessons could be adapted for one-to-one remediation of students with language disorders or learning disabilities.

BACKGROUND

Language Strategies for Little Ones is based on several educational models, principles, and philosophies that address the needs of the learner as a whole. These premises are embedded within the lessons and are summarized in the following sections.

Repeated Exposure

Caine and Caine (1991), Kavalic and Olsen (1993), and Hunter (1982) describe natural brain functioning and the implications for the teaching process. The teaching principles suggested by these researchers stress the total emotional, physiological, and psychological involvement of the brain in the learning process, particularly the need to pair familiarity with novelty and challenge and the need for repeated exposure. The brain's search for meaning through "patterning" (i.e., patterns connect new knowledge to prior experience) is an important learning component (Caine and Caine, 1991; Kavalic and Olsen, 1993).

Multisensory Methods

Rief (1993) reports that the majority of students are visual and tactile/kinesthetic learners. She cautions, "Only 15 percent tend to be strong auditory learners. If your teaching style emphasizes lecturing, with you doing all the talking, there is a high percentage of students you're not reaching... We need to present lessons with a combination of methods" (p. 53). The lessons in *Language Strategies for Little Ones* provide a variety of activities, so students can find their own avenues for success in language learning. Sounds, words, or rhymes are highlighted to engage the auditory learner. Visual learners have the benefit of a visual aid or graphic representation of the strategy. Clapping, tracing, and gesturing are utilized for the tactile/kinesthetic learner. Children have opportunities for pragmatic practice in both large and small group activities. Other subject areas can be integrated into the lessons to draw on potential student strengths. For example, while learning to use question words in the social application story *Use Your Question Words!* students also learn the life cycle of the butterfly.

Strategy-Based Intervention

The lessons in *Language Strategies for Little Ones* are facilitated by easy-to-remember learning strategies. Cognitive (e.g., analyzing) and metacognitive (e.g., planning and organizing) strategies are important to effective language learning (Oxford, 1994). Strategies should fit learning styles (i.e., they should be multisensory to meet the needs of visual symbolizers as well as auditory symbolizers [McInroy, 1996]). There should be plenty of opportunities for practicing the learning strategies during the lessons. The teaching of strategies should include explanations, handouts, activities, and home-practice materials (Oxford, 1994). Each strategy in this resource has an accompanying visual graphic for remembering it, activities for learning it, an opportunity for demonstrating it, and homework activities for introducing it to families.

Some of the strategies included require students to self-evaluate and self-monitor their communication breakdowns in social situations (e.g., when talking with friends) or at school (e.g., when listening to the teacher or working on group projects). For those learners who find vocabulary or concepts in classroom curricula challenging, the strategies provide a plan for repairing interactions when breakdowns occur.

Whole Language Philosophy

Whole language has been described as a partnership between intent and learning, focusing on meaning and relevancy as the catalyst for learning (Wagner, 1989). Whole language capitalizes on the social aspects of communication in which the language learner strives to bridge experiences and understanding (Genishi, 1988). While the whole language philosophy is not applied in its purest form in *Language Strategies for Little Ones*, language learning is addressed in context, as it occurs, in "language-loaded" situations. Lessons integrate listening, speaking, reading, and writing at a level appropriate to the student.

Curriculum-Based Intervention

Intervention that integrates curriculum vocabulary and concepts with communication goals is termed *curriculum-based intervention* (A. Bird, personal communication, September 1, 1992). This approach to intervention creates a relevant context for language learning. *Language Strategies for Little Ones* is curriculum-based. For example, in *Hit the Bull's-Eye: Giving and Receiving Directions,* a pond scene is used to practice using clear, specific language when giving directions. The message sender chooses from a number of pictures (e.g., a big and a small cloud, tall and short trees, two different-colored kites) and gives directions to a partner for placement on the pond scene. Concepts and vocabulary for this activity include *above, below, next to, beside, over, under, right, left, top, bottom, land, pond, sky,* and so on. This activity clearly emphasizes using specific language and requesting clarification when further information is needed. It is important to keep in mind that curriculum-based intervention emphasizes communication goals but uses curricular concepts as the stimuli for improving communication. Educators should adapt activities by embedding their district's curricular goals and objectives into the lessons.

Literature-Based Intervention

Language Strategies for Little Ones embeds high-interest literature, which is an engaging, entertaining format for learning communication. For example, *Who Is the Beast?* (1990), by Keith Baker, lends itself to teaching attributes of animals, as well as comparing and contrasting. The story describes a number of jungle animals by specific features. The students discover how the animals are alike in certain ways and how they are different in other ways, and they capture this information in a Venn diagram graphic (see *Alike and Different Lily Pads [Part I]*). *Language Strategies for Little Ones* lessons incorporate literature that can be linked to the classroom curriculum. The literature used in *Language Strategies for Little Ones* is listed in the bibliography.

PROGRAM COMPONENTS

Lessons

Hunter's (1982) lesson cycle format reinforces the principles of brain-based research by providing repeated exposure to a concept within a lesson. Hunter describes the lesson components that she feels maximize learning on the part of the student. Primary lesson components include the following:

1. *Objectives*—describe the change in student behavior that is desired
2. *Anticipatory Set*—sets the stage for learning by sparking student interest and curiosity about the lesson
3. *Modeling*—presents examples of behaviors the educator wants the students to perform independently
4. *Guided Practice*—checks the students' level of understanding of the concept before moving on
5. *Independent Practice*—provides tasks to be completed until students show mastery of the lesson concepts or skills

The lesson format used in *Language Strategies for Little Ones* is an adaptation of Hunter's (1982) model. In addition to *Goal, Background Information,* and *Materials,* every lesson includes the following components:

1. *Objectives*—The objectives clearly state the change expected in students' behavior within each lesson, although measurable elements should be added based on each student's needs.
2. *Introduction*—The introduction parallels the anticipatory set of Hunter's (1982) model. It has two elements, *tie-in to prior learning* and *focus/relevancy*. The *tie-in to prior learning* section is a review of the previous lesson (if appropriate). It sets the stage for connecting prior experience with new knowledge. The *focus/relevancy* section establishes an anticipatory set. Therefore, more meaningful or vivid entry into a topic results. Focusing techniques include a proposal of a provocative question or a statement of the objective. The purpose of this component is to have students clear their minds of irrelevant ideas and be ready to learn, especially since they know what it is they are to focus on and what they are expected to learn.
3. *Lesson Activities*—The lesson activities present the basic information necessary to meet the objectives. Modeling the strategy or process is essential to ensuring understanding. Hunter (1982) stresses the use of key words and simple diagrams in a lesson, and these techniques are what comprise the language strategies presented. Each lesson activity includes checking for understanding, including signaled answers, choral responses, or a sampling of individual responses (either oral or written).
4. *Closure*—The closure activity includes a discussion of the lesson relevance and value. *Teaching for transfer,* as Hunter (1982) calls it, involves making the information meaningful by connecting past and future knowledge to present learning. The educator identifies critical parts of the present learning and ties it to the child's life, using techniques such as mnemonics or memory helpers. *Teaching for meaning* (i.e., introducing short, meaningful "chunks" of information for students to practice), as Hunter terms it, is included through guided and independent practice.

Lessons also apply the principle of *distributed practice* in that strategies previously taught are revisited periodically as they apply to a current lesson. This method helps to improve retention of the strategy. For example, the lesson on using question words to gain information is continually reinforced whenever students need to acquire new information by asking questions.

Strategy Graphics

Each strategy has a graphic as a visual aid. The graphic should be duplicated and enlarged to create a poster. The poster can be colored, mounted onto colorful construction paper or poster board, and laminated for durability. It should be posted on a classroom wall or bulletin board and referred to while students are learning the strategy or when the strategy is reviewed. The posters can also be used to generalize strategy use when teaching curricular concepts throughout the day.

The graphic can also be used to create transparencies for overhead projectors. For example, in the *Alike and Different Lily Pads* lesson, the educator could use the transparency to write on while comparing and contrasting two objects or concepts.

Social Application Stories

Social application stories are included periodically to provide a concrete representation of the value of the targeted strategies. The pages can be enlarged and colored to make a big book or duplicated for each student and cut along the dotted line to make smaller books for them to color. Simply staple the pages together to form the books.

These stories introduce the characters of Professor Green, the teacher frog, and Einstein, the young frog who is learning valuable skills. For example, in the story that stresses the value of good listening, Einstein learns that when he stops, listens, and concentrates, he is able to identify sounds in his environment that bring rewards, keep him safe, and help him learn. Student interest is captured by the entertaining, predictable stories. Even a nonreader can "read along" with the class!

Skills Checklists

Language Strategies for Little Ones introduces students to taking responsibility for and ownership of their communication goals. The students contribute to this process by checking off what they have learned on a page called *Skills Checklist*.

Using skills checklists is an extremely successful teaching strategy that helps students feel informed about their learning and progress. Checklists lead students to be more enthusiastic and motivated to learn.

Homework Activities

Homework activities are provided for each strategy so that students can share the targeted skill with their families. The activities have students share the strategies with their family members and then apply them to several tasks at home. After students complete the activities, family members are asked to sign and date the sheets and then return them to school. Establishing a reward system for completing the activities and returning signed sheets helps to ensure that this important step is done.

The activities encourage family involvement and demonstrate how home practice can support communication skills in a quick, easy, and useful way. Students learn that their family members value good communication skills

Communication Skills Newsletters

After several lessons have been taught, a newsletter explaining the strategies, vocabulary, and activities covered in class should be sent home to family members. The newsletters provide a nice bridge between the classroom and home, so parents can be involved in their children's learning.

Portfolios

For this resource, skills checklists, returned homework activities pages, and anecdotal information regarding progress or concerns comprise the students' portfolios. The educator should collect these items, as well as relevant classroom work, to keep in the portfolios. Anecdotal notes from a variety of teachers are a valuable source of documentation of progress as the child moves from grade to grade. The notes could give specific examples of when students apply strategies (e.g., a teacher may document that on 10/15, when Jimmy was supposed to raise his hand to ask a question, he would tell about an event instead, but that on 3/15, Jimmy was using all of his question words to gather information). These anecdotes may also be obtained by briefly interviewing teachers regarding their observations of a student's growth over time.

Educator-created checklists to itemize desired communication skills or strategy use may also be used to assess progress informally. A child's current performance may be compared to his or her previous performances (work samples, pre- and posttesting, and anecdotal information) to show change over time. Portfolio collections should be shared with family members at annual meetings or parent-teacher conferences.

Vacation Calendar

Language Strategies for Little Ones includes a *Vacation Calendar.* The calendar includes two months worth of activities that can be done in five minutes or less on a daily basis at home. If using the calendar in a "traditional," nine-month school year, the activities could be completed during the summer months. If using the calendar in a year-round school district, the calendar is easily adapted to accommodate such a schedule.

The months and dates are purposely not included on the calendar to allow flexibility, but should be added before duplicating for students. Educators should recommend to students, or to family members at an annual review meeting or conference, that the calendar be hung on the refrigerator (or some other prominent spot) and worked on at a specific time each day (e.g., breakfast or bedtime). Parents or caregivers should initial each daily activity when it is completed. A reward for completed and initialed calendars may be offered at the beginning of the return to school.

PROCEDURES FOR USE

Language Strategies for Little Ones is written as a starting point for educators who will develop lessons using their own style of teaching. It provides a framework that a beginning professional can follow or one that an experienced teacher can incorporate into a previously existing program. The lessons will spur new ideas.

Units and Goals

Language Strategies for Little Ones is divided into three main units: (1) language comprehension, (2) oral expression, and (3) story grammar knowledge.

1. *Language Comprehension*—addresses the listening process by

    - making the student aware of the difference between hearing and listening (i.e., one can hear sounds in the environment, but until the brain is engaged, no meaning is attached to the sound source)
    - discussing what can interfere (both intrinsically and extrinsically) with the listening process
    - discussing what to do in distracting situations
    - building active listening skills during lessons (The students are frequently given a listening job [i.e., told to listen for specific information or words] to keep them involved and focused.)
    - stressing evaluative thinking (The lessons create opportunities for students to recognize the need for clarification, as well as how to ask for clarification appropriately.)
    - applying evaluative listening and thinking skills to differentiate between real and pretend events, objects, or characters in a variety of contexts
    - emphasizing the comprehension and use of precise and specific language terms in communication (e.g., *below, above, beside, near, far, in, out*)

2. *Oral Expression*—addresses the speaking process by
    - stressing the use of the five senses to describe objects, pictures, and events
    - discussing the use of descriptive language in creating a more vivid message for the listener (or reader, if written)
    - discussing the need to make scientific observations and to verbally share discoveries with other observers on a team
    - introducing the use of language skills in problem solving and higher level thinking (e.g., categorizing, comparing and contrasting)
    - developing "word play," or vocabulary knowledge and flexibility in word use (e.g., producing regular and irregular past tense verbs, using descriptive words, understanding multiple meanings of words), for use in manipulating language meaning
3. *Story Grammar Knowledge*—addresses narrative language skills by
    - providing a guideline of story grammar elements
    - stressing the use of a story grammar framework for relaying a personal experience or generating or retelling a fictional story
    - applying story grammar strategies to oral and written language
    - emphasizing the need to tell the important points rather than retelling an entire story when giving the main idea
    - applying evaluative listening/thinking skills to link information and recognize the parts of a cause/effect relationship

Communication objectives are organized within these three units. Lessons clearly emphasize one of the areas; however, in keeping with the philosophy of whole language, all areas of communication are integrated within lessons (i.e., a lesson with a listening goal may also contain objectives with a speaking focus).

The Cross-Reference Chart (see page 15) lists the objectives covered in each lesson. While several objectives are targeted specifically, a number of objectives are indirectly developed as well. In this way, the lessons build upon one another, with previous objectives reviewed and reinforced in subsequent lessons. This repetition also accommodates the needs of students who enter the program at different times and may have missed earlier lessons.

Presenting the Lesson

The lessons are presented for use in a classroom setting; however, they are easily adapted for smaller groups by allowing more individual responses and participation. Using the lessons within a small group setting allows the educator to spend whatever time is necessary to ensure that all students have an understanding of the targeted objectives. A small group setting also provides more opportunities for independent practice.

Lessons are intended for students in kindergarten and first grade. Content should be expanded and modified within each lesson to fit the particular levels of the students. The use of higher level questioning can be used to extend any lesson. Bloom's (1956) taxonomy lists a hierarchy of questioning difficulty, beginning at the knowledge level, where only content questions are asked (e.g., "What was the name of the main character?" "Who was at the party?"). Questions requiring more thought to respond and questions that require students to manipulate information, arrive at conclusions, or draw inferences (e.g., "Why did John decide to leave?" "Do you think he made a good choice?" "Why or why not?" "What else could he have chosen to do?") should be asked to expand the lesson as appropriate.

Most lessons can be taught within a 30-minute class period. However, lessons can be extended over several class periods to ensure understanding or to give students more opportunities to practice a new strategy. Lessons with more than one activity may require more than one session to complete.

Hints are included in many of the lessons to provide helpful information or suggestions for adapting the lessons in different ways. The hints also facilitate the flow of the lesson and are provided to help prevent potential problems.

Suggestions for using literature are included and are referred to as *literary highlights*. They are often included when a piece of literature, listed in the *Materials* section, is used with the lesson. When using any type of literature, the author, illustrator, book cover, and any relevant vocabulary should be discussed. Note particular components of the book (e.g., a figurative language expression or multiple meaning words) *while* reading the story, rather than discussing them out of context *before* reading the story. Suggestions are provided for before, during, and/or after story reading. If substituting another book, adapt the suggestions for the selected book.

Before beginning any lesson, materials should be gathered. This includes creating the strategy poster, which provides a visual cue for students to remember each targeted strategy. It is an integral part of the lesson and can be referred to in subsequent lessons. The educator should duplicate and enlarge the graphic, color it, mount it onto colorful construction paper or poster board, and laminate it for durability, if desired. Certain lessons will require the students or educator to write on the poster itself. If laminating is not an option, an overhead transparency of the strategy would allow words to be written on it and erased easily. Certain parts of the lessons require writing information where all students can see it. In the *Materials* section, chalk and chalkboard are listed as the medium for writing the information, but markers and a dry erase board or an overhead projector works just as well.

Certain parts of the lessons have been scripted to give the educator an example of presenting the idea. The scripts are examples only and should be reworded to fit the educator's teaching style and the students' learning needs. For example, scripts in the *focus/relevancy* section of the lessons are intended to lure students into the lesson so that they are curious, excited, ready to problem solve, and immediately engaged in the lesson. The educator may opt for a more direct focus by simply stating the purpose of the lesson.

It is preferable that the educator find (or order from the publisher, Thinking Publications) a frog puppet or stuffed frog to represent the Einstein character from the social application stories and lessons. The Einstein character is used during the *tie-in to prior learning* or *focus/relevancy* sections of the lessons to teach or remind the students of salient information. If the educator does not choose to manipulate an Einstein character, he or she will need to take on that role within those portions of the lessons where Einstein is used. Use of a character or theme is motivating and useful. While speaking to Einstein, younger students will often practice skills they might hesitate to voice in other situations (e.g., while practicing their use of question words, students enjoy "interviewing" Einstein to gain information or knowledge). They enjoy analogies made between the frog's home and their own and relate to the young language-learning character.

Homework activities are provided so that the students can share the targeted strategies and skills with their families. The activities generally ask the students to summarize the strategy and apply it to a home or community situation (e.g., for *categorizing*, the students may be asked to help Mom sort the groceries into pantry or refrigerated groups). This encourages parent/child involvement and gives family members examples of how home practice can support communication skills in a quick, easy way.

Additional Techniques

To ensure the participation of all students within the groups, and to keep students engaged during the activity or during a brief discussion portion of the lesson, it is recommended that the educator employ a variety of techniques. The following techniques, occasionally mentioned within the lessons, have been found to be useful when teaching in an inclusion-model classroom:

1. *Golf Clap*—The golf clap involves tapping the first two fingers on the palm of the opposite hand. This virtually noiseless clap can be used by an entire class to clap out the syllables in a

multisyllabic word that is difficult to pronounce. It can also be used to show understanding of a concept, as when one student has been called on to give an answer, other students can indicate that they were thinking of the same answer by using their golf clap. The educator can keep more students engaged by acknowledging those students signaling identical responses with their golf clap (e.g., "I see John and Sara were thinking of the same answer as Antonio"). The educator may extend responses by asking for different answers or ideas.

2. *Brainstorming*—Brainstorming involves having students generate as many ideas as possible. Ideas are not judged as appropriate or inappropriate when brainstorming, because implausible responses can generate alternatives.

3. *Choral Response*—Choral responses are done in unison as a group. This can be done while answering questions or completing a cloze procedure sentence (e.g., while reviewing a new concept, the educator might prompt, "When I tell the size, I'm using..." [choral response] "word power"). While reading a predictable portion of a story, the whole class can help read the repetitive portions (e.g., "Oh, that's bad!" in *That's Good! That's Bad!*).

4. *Signaling*—Systematic responses should be established in order to demonstrate agreement or disagreement according to the educator's directions (e.g., giving the thumbs-up signal).

5. *Role-Playing*—The educator has the students act out, or pantomime, the information being discussed (e.g., the educator has the students use body language to show that they are bored and then has them use it to show that they are excited, as if someone just brought in cupcakes).

6. *Gesturing*—The students use hand/body movements to illustrate the concept discussed (e.g., making a lasso with their arms rounded into a circle to emphasize the notion of grouping items into categories, or showing with their bodies the difference between high/low, big/small, in/out, hot/cold, etc. when learning about opposites).

7. *Whisper Voices*—The whisper voice is used when the entire classroom is responding in unison in a choral response. The whisper voice minimizes disruption or disturbance of nearby classrooms.

8. *Six-Inch Voices*—Using six-inch voices is a way to describe the volume students should use when working in small groups or pairs. Six-inch voices can only be heard within six inches of the speaker. This technique helps to keep the volume level in the classroom manageable.

9. *Learning Groups*—For maximum student participation, many activities suggest that students work in small groups. If the educator is versed in the principles of cooperative learning (Johnson, Johnson, and Johnson Holubec, 1990; Kagan, 1994), these principles can be applied.

For example, students could be paired with one person designated as A and one as B. The educator may then ask the As to share with the Bs, and vice versa, as a discussion method that ensures that all students are participating. Another example of pairing might be giving each child a stimulus card and having them ask their neighbors what is on their card, trying to make a logical connection, such as *cow* and *barn*. The educator may have the pairs come up before the others to explain why their words go together. When working in small groups, one student can act as a recorder and another as a reporter. The recorder writes or marks in some way the group's ideas, and the reporter shares the ideas with the large group. These roles can be assigned by the educator by saying something like, "Today the students wearing the most blue will be the recorders, and the students wearing the most brown will be the reporters." This type of strategy gives all group members the opportunity to participate in each role.

CROSS-REFERENCE CHART

The chart on page 15 provides a cross-reference of lessons or strategies and communication goals or objectives. The chart lists the lessons/strategies and goals/objectives targeted within the lessons. (Objectives are stated more specifically within the lessons.) The chart also lists objectives that are indirectly targeted within the lessons. Use this cross-reference to develop goals and objectives for students' individualized educational programs (IEPs) if desired. To use objectives for IEPs, measurable components should be added to them.

Cross-Reference Chart

GOALS/OBJECTIVES — LESSONS/STRATEGIES	UNIT 1	Give Me Five	CAREful Listening	Clarifying with Question Words	Hit the Bull's-Eye	UNIT 2	It Makes Sense: Sight Words	It Makes Sense: Sound Words	It Makes Sense: Taste/Smell Words	It Makes Sense: Touch Words	Symbols Have Meaning	Lasso the Word Herd	Say It Another Way	Alike and Different Lily Pads	Learning about Opposites	Discover the Pattern	Picture a Clear Definition	UNIT 3	Story Recipe	Follow the Detail Trail	Tell the Biggest Eggs	Why? Because!
Listening Actively		x	x	x	x		x	•	•	•	•	•	•	•	•	•	•		•	•	•	•
Drawing Conclusions		•	•	•	•		x		x	x		x	x		•	x			•	•	•	•
Requesting Clarification			x	x	x																	
Making Associations (Comparing and Contrasting)			•				•	•	•	•	x	x	•	x	x	x	x					
Recognizing and Using Question Words				x	x		•	•	•	•					•	•	•					
Giving Attributes				•	x		•	•	•	•	•	•	•	x	•	x	x			•		
Categorizing												x		x	•	x	x					
Giving Synonyms			•										x	•	x	x	•					
Giving Antonyms															x	x	•					
Solving Analogies																x						
Sequencing Events													•						x	x	•	•
Recognizing/Telling Cause and Effect											•		•	•	•				•	•	x	x
Recognizing and Applying Story Construction																			x	x	•	•
Recognizing and Applying the 5 Senses			•				x	x	x	x						•						
Telling Main Idea														•					•	•	x	•
Explaining/Using Figurative Language		•	•										x	•					•	•		
Making Pragmatic Decisions (Using Social Language)		•	•	x	x									•		•			•			
Demonstrating Knowledge Orally		•	x	x	x		x	x	x	x	x	x	x	x	x	x	x		x	x	x	x
Demonstrating Knowledge in Written Language				•				•		•	•	•		•								•

x = Targeted objective • = Additional skill that is "touched on" within the lesson

UNIT ONE

GIVE ME FIVE: STOP AND LISTEN (PART I)

GOAL

To improve listening skills

BACKGROUND INFORMATION

The *Give Me Five: Stop and Listen* strategy addresses listening versus hearing, use of appropriate listening body language, and key words and phrases to signal the need to listen. The main focus of this lesson is to provide students with a strategy that helps them be prepared and attentive for the task of listening. We all "drop out" of listening situations from time to time, but if we don't bring ourselves back, we can lose track of what is being said. The "give me five" signal can be used by educators to bring students to attention and can help students bring themselves back to a listening situation.

Be aware of the misconception that good listeners keep their eyes focused on the speaker at all times (Jalongo, 1991). Although the *Give Me Five* strategy does ask students to keep their eyes on the speaker, the strategy is used to focus attention, rather than to get students to maintain eye contact throughout the listening situation. Also be aware that cultural expectations for listening behaviors may differ.

Social application stories are included periodically to illustrate the value of the targeted strategies. The stories use a predictable pattern and reinforce abstract concepts (e.g., the importance of listening, word power, and story grammar knowledge).

The Einstein character is used during the *tie-in to prior learning* or *focus/relevancy* sections to teach the students or remind the students of salient information. If the educator does not choose to manipulate an Einstein character, he or she will need to take on that role within those portions of the lessons where Einstein is used.

HINT

It is strongly recommended that the educator read the *presenting the lesson* and *additional techniques* sections of *Procedures for Use.* Suggestions for maximizing participation and learning are offered that may be applied throughout the program.

OBJECTIVES

1. Tell how listening differs from hearing.
2. State the importance of listening, as opposed to hearing, to gain knowledge in learning and play situations, as well as for safety reasons.
3. Use appropriate body language for listening: eyes on the speaker, mouth quiet, body still, ears listening, and hands free.

MATERIALS

1. Einstein character (Recommended but not necessary; see page 12.)
2. Social application story: *Einstein Learns about Listening* (See pages 23–29; also see page 7.)
3. *Give Me Five* graphic (See page 30; duplicate and enlarge the graphic, color it, mount it onto colorful construction paper or poster board, and laminate it for durability, if desired.)

INTRODUCTION

Tie-in to Prior Learning

Prompt the students to brainstorm listening experiences they may have had today at school (e.g., the teacher asking them to listen) and at home (e.g., listening to instructions for getting dressed).

Focus/Relevancy

1. Ask the students if they think that listening is an important skill. Show the cover of the social application story, featuring Einstein and Professor Green. Explain that these characters will help them learn special skills to become better listeners and speakers. Introduce the Einstein character if you are using one, and allow time for all students to say "Hi" to Einstein.

2. Explain how Einstein learns to improve his listening by stopping and listening with his whole body. (Show the *Give Me Five* poster.) Ask the students how Einstein uses his whole body to listen. Point out the symbols for keeping their eyes on speaker, mouth quiet, body still, ears listening, and hands free. Ask what other part of his body helps him listen. Elicit the need to use the brain to identify the sounds we hear.

3. Read the social application story *Einstein Learns about Listening* (see pages 23–29). Discuss the lessons that Einstein learns:

   a. Einstein learns to listen to get a special treat. Let the students share their own experiences of when listening has helped them get a special treat (e.g., recognizing the sound of an ice-cream truck or getting to go to recess early because everyone listened to the teacher).

   b. Einstein learns to be safe by listening to avoid being run over by a big machine. Let students discuss how listening can help keep them safe at home, at school, and in the community (e.g., while crossing the street, during fire drills, and when encountering sirens).

   c. Einstein learns to swim by listening to his coach. Discuss the importance of listening to a coach, teacher, or dance instructor, for instance, to become a more skillful player, student, or dancer.

LESSON ACTIVITIES

1. Describe to the students the difference between hearing and listening. Explain that there are constantly sounds around us but that we may not be aware of them. Pair up students and have them decide who will be A and who will be B (see page 14). Have the student pairs sit quietly for a few moments to listen to and identify some of the sounds they hear around them. Then ask student A to tell student B what was different when they *listened*. Allow one minute for A to share without being interrupted. Then have student B share for one minute. Summarize the insight that the sounds around them were there all along but that until the brain was engaged, the listener was not always aware of them; the sounds had no meaning. When we need to listen for meaning, the brain has to be engaged.

2. Share your observations of how during Activity 1, when the students were pausing to listen, their body language showed that their brain was engaged and that listening was taking place. Give examples of the different styles of body language that were exhibited (e.g., some students were still, some were quiet, some students looked down, others looked at the teacher or around the room).

   A fun way to explore body language is to role-play various scenarios. Have the students slouch in their seat as if they were bored. Then have them pretend that someone has brought in a tray of cupcakes. Let the students show their change in feelings through their body language. Comment on how excited they appear when they sit up, raise their eyebrows, and smile. Contrast the cupcake scenario to someone bringing in a tray of rotten fruit. Allow time for students to respond to the latter example, and comment on the changes made in their appearance (e.g., frowns, scowls, turning away).

3. Show the *Give Me Five* poster, and make the gesture of an outstretched palm with your fingers pointing up. Explain what the symbols mean (i.e., eyes on the speaker, mouth quiet, body still, ears listening, and hands free). Connect the idea of body awareness to listening effectively.

   Tell the students that they are going to practice Einstein's *Give Me Five* strategy. A fun way to explain each of the *Give Me Five* rules is through role-playing examples of different listening situations. Have Einstein lead the students in practicing the following:

   - *Eyes on the speaker*—Einstein or the educator can note that the students are already demonstrating this skill by the way they are watching whenever the "give me five" signal is given. Explain that the speaker may not always be the teacher (e.g., the speaker may be a student, a parent, or a visitor) and that listening rules still apply. Once students know the listening job, it may no longer be necessary for them to keep their eyes continuously on the speaker, although it may help to keep them focused on the information being given.

- *Mouth quiet*—Have the children role-play students talking who must stop upon seeing or hearing the "give me five" signal. Compliment the students on how quickly they demonstrate the *Give Me Five* rules. Describe how during some listening tasks, the listener may think of events to share, but may have to wait until a later time to share them. For example, if a student has a lot of knowledge about dinosaurs and the story is about Tyrannosaurus rex, he or she may have some expert information to share that will have to wait for another time. The story may make the student think about a fun trip to a place having to do with dinosaurs, but once again, he or she has to wait for the right time to share the story.
- *Body still*—Have the group twist or wiggle in their seats. After displaying the "give me five" signal, have the students stop all body movement and sit up straight and tall. Explain how body movements and posture can affect how well the student and those around him or her listen. Have students demonstrate possible body positions appropriate for longer listening tasks (e.g., lying on the floor, standing beside their desk, or resting their head on their desk). Note, however, that constantly changing from one position to another is distracting for the listener and his or her neighbors.
- *Ears listening*—Review the difference between simply hearing sounds and listening by using the brain to identify the sound or message. Refer to the discussion from Activity 1.
- *Hands free*—Einstein or the educator should have the entire group act out cutting or writing. When the educator gives the "give me five" signal while saying "Give me five," the students should immediately stop what they are doing, put down their pretend materials, and give the "give me five" signal. Role-play again. Have the students pretend to listen to a story while being distracted by their really neat, new sports pencil. Have the students demonstrate ways to return to the listening job (e.g., putting the pretend pencil away or purposely directing their attention to the speaker).

CLOSURE

Summarize the lesson, repeat its relevance to students, and tie it to future learning. Have students tell why it is important to be prepared to listen, and review the *Give Me Five* poster. Brainstorm other classroom or home situations where appropriate listening body language is beneficial. Use the "give me five" signal throughout the day as a way to gain students' attention (e.g., while lining up for recess or lunch, when giving instructions, when giving important information pertaining to assignments and/or homework). Ultimately, this signal can be used at any time during any activity throughout the school year as a method to quickly gain children's attention. In Part II of this lesson, students will listen and then signal when they hear target words.

Listening is an important skill...

You can hear many sounds around you!

When you listen with your brain you can tell what each sound is!

2

What do I hear?

3

4

Listening with my brain got me a special treat.

5

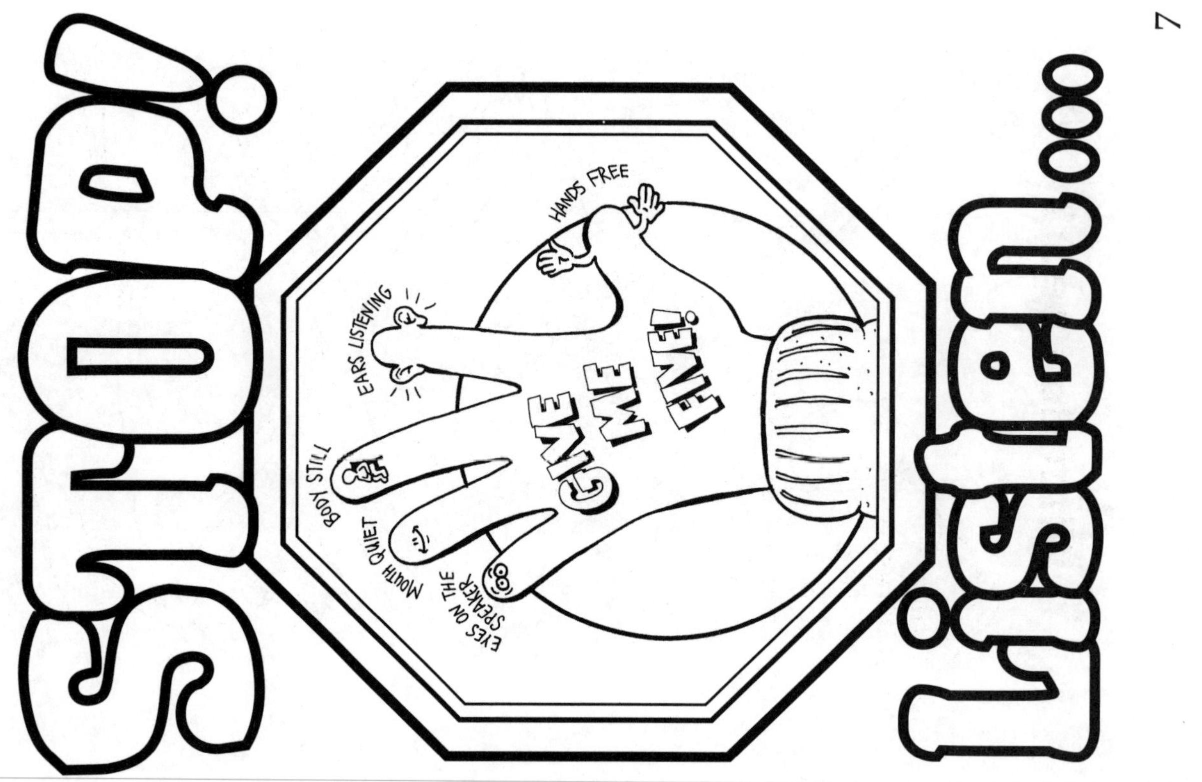
STOP!
EYES ON THE SPEAKER
MOUTH QUIET
BODY STILL
EARS LISTENING
HANDS FREE
GIVE ME FIVE!
Listen...
7

What do I hear?
Rattle, Rattle, Clatter
6

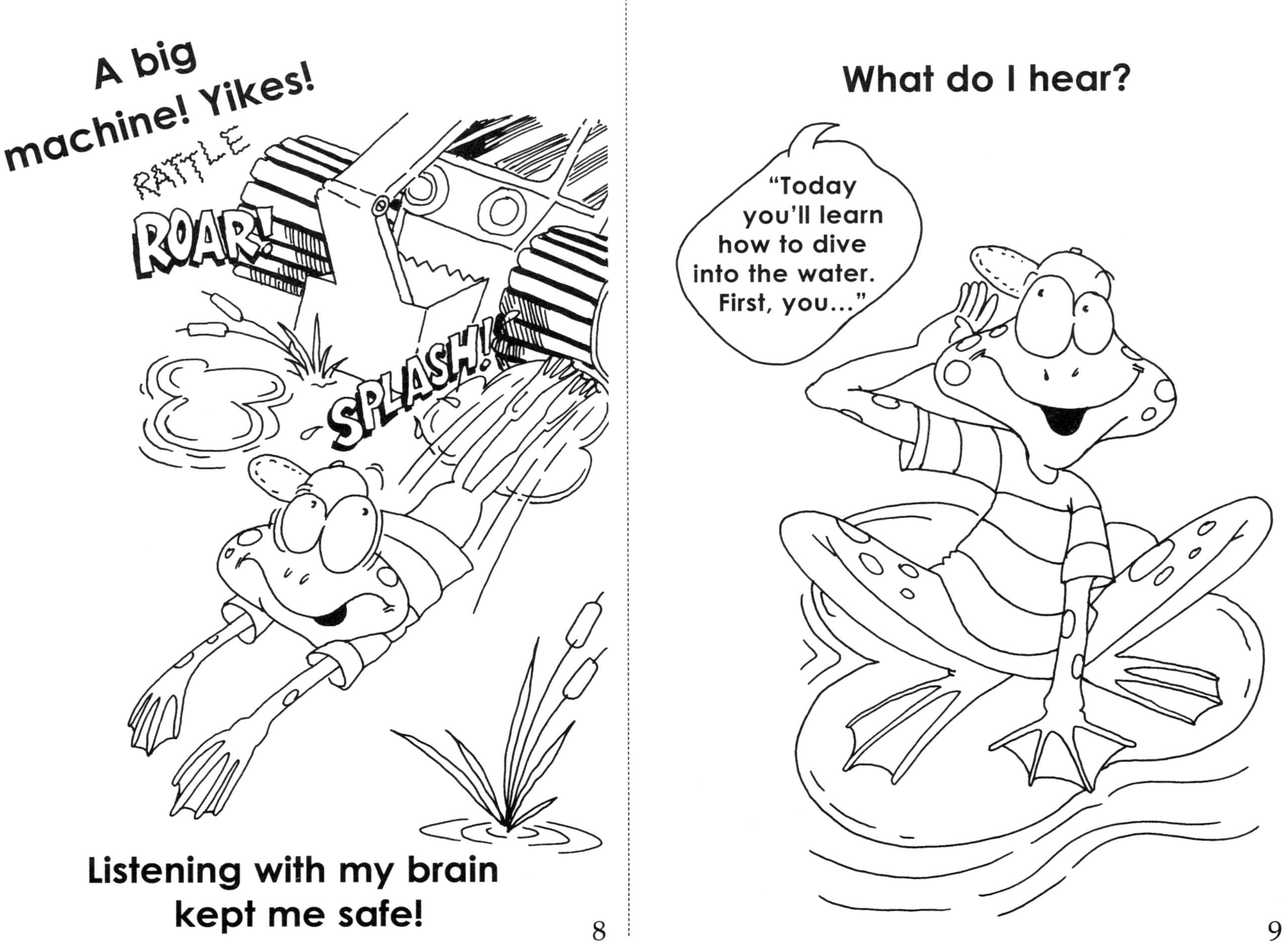
A big machine! Yikes!
RATTLE
ROAR!
SPLASH!
Listening with my brain kept me safe!
8
What do I hear?
"Today you'll learn how to dive into the water. First, you…"
9

STOP!
EYES ON THE SPEAKER
MOUTH QUIET
BODY STILL
EARS LISTENING
HANDS FREE
GIVE ME FIVE!
Listen...
10

The teacher! I know what to do!
Listening with my brain
helped me learn!
Swim Team
Practice
M-F 9-11:00
COACH
11

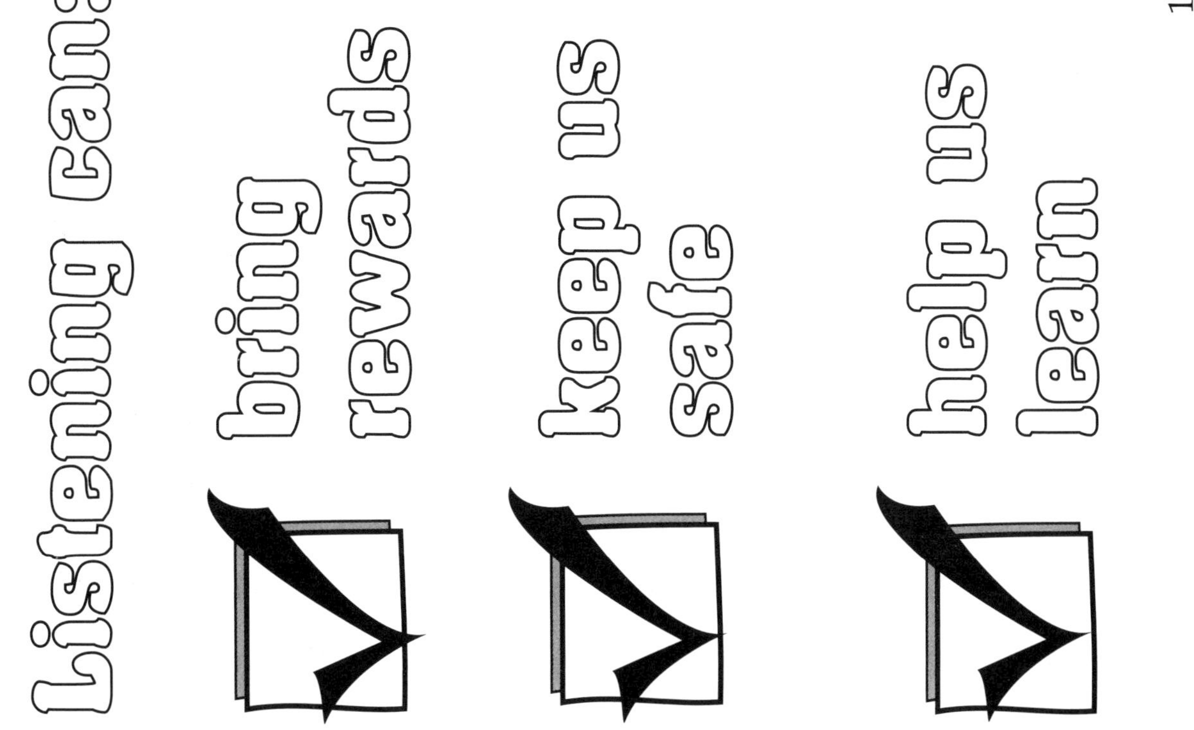
Listening can:
bring rewards
keep us safe
help us learn
12

STOP!
BODY STILL
MOUTH QUIET
EARS LISTENING
EYES ON THE SPEAKER
HANDS FREE
GIVE ME FIVE!
Listen...

GIVE ME FIVE: STOP AND LISTEN (PART II)

GOAL

To improve listening skills

BACKGROUND INFORMATION

The *Give Me Five: Stop and Listen* strategy addresses listening versus hearing, use of appropriate listening body language, and key words and phrases to signal the need to listen. The main focus of this lesson is to provide students with a strategy that helps them be prepared and attentive for the task of listening. We all "drop out" of listening situations from time to time, but if we don't bring ourselves back, we can lose track of what is being said. The "give me five" signal can be used by educators to bring students to attention and can help students bring themselves back to a listening situation. In this lesson, students will be given an active listening job to keep them alert and listening throughout a story.

OBJECTIVES

1. Use appropriate body language—eyes on the speaker, mouth quiet, body still, ears listening, and hands free—during a longer listening situation.
2. Listen and then signal when specific sound words are read within a story.

MATERIALS

1. Einstein character (Recommended but not necessary; see page 12.)
2. Social application story: *Einstein Learns about Listening* (Created earlier)
3. *Let's Go Home, Little Bear* (1993), by Martin Waddell, illustrated by Barbara Firth (If desired, substitute another book such as *The Happy Hedgehog Band,* 1992, by Martin Waddell, illustrated by Jill Barton. It is preferable that the book have sound words or objects that might make sounds [e.g., in this story, the bear hears such sounds as "plodding" and "creaking"]. It is more enjoyable if the sound words do not match the students' prediction of the sound source.)
4. *Give Me Five* poster (Created earlier)

INTRODUCTION

Tie-in to Prior Learning

Have Einstein ask the students if they can remember why it is important even for frogs to be good listeners. Review the list of reasons from the *Einstein Learns about Listening* summary page depicting a checklist of positive outcomes for listening (i.e., rewards, safety, learning) as a review from the previous lesson (see page 29).

Focus/Relevancy

Have Einstein explain how it takes practice to be a good listener. Ask the students to give the thumbs-up signal if they think that listening is an important skill for children too.

To allow the students to share how listening is important in their lives, use the A/B pair discussion technique (see page 14). Let Einstein explain that sometimes it is hard to listen for a long time. He can tell a story about having to listen at frog school when Professor Green was teaching about ways to keep the pond pollution free. He talked for a long time, and Einstein had to work hard not to daydream about going swimming.

LESSON ACTIVITIES

1. Show the book *Let's Go Home, Little Bear* (1993), by Martin Waddell, illustrated by Barbara Firth. Point out the following literary highlights:
   - Book cover. (Discuss: What season does it show? How do they know? Do the students think the story is real or pretend?)
   - Vocabulary—*plod, glance, path, stream, cave, embers, cozy* (Discuss/demonstrate what plodding would look like; let students pretend to walk in deep snow.)
   - Multiple meaning words—*stirred, track, feet, stream, down, back, lap*

   NOTE: Discuss vocabulary, multiple meaning words, expressions, etc. while, rather then before or after, reading the story.
2. Introduce the students' next listening task by discussing the importance of listening for key words or phrases teachers or speakers often use to signal an important message. When the students hear certain words or phrases such as "Give me five," "This is important," or "I hope you're listening carefully," the students should immediately demonstrate appropriate listening body language (see page 18). Explain that there will be times when students will need to actively listen for extended periods of time. The students may have to give themselves reminders to keep listening, just as they did when they role-played being distracted by their pencils and then ignoring the distraction.
3. Introduce the active listening task in which the students give the thumbs-up signal when they hear the following sound words:

a. *plod, plod, plod*

b. *drip, drip, drip*

c. *plop, plop, plop*

d. *woo, woo, woo*

e. *creak, creak, creak*

Have the students predict or guess what might be making each of the targeted sounds. Make the activity more fun by telling students that you will try to trick them if they are not really careful listeners!

These sound words are specific examples from the *Let's Go Home, Little Bear* story. If substituting another book, look for specific words that students must listen for. It is preferable that the book have sound words or objects that might make sounds.

4. Read the story. As each sound word is read, praise the students' use of active listening as indicated by the thumbs-up signal. Call on students sitting quietly with their hand raised to tell how the sources of the sounds used in the story were different from the students' predictions. Show the *Give Me Five* poster. Ask several students to tell how they used the *Give Me Five: Stop and Listen* strategy to maintain appropriate listening body language throughout the story.

CLOSURE

Summarize the lesson, repeat its relevance to students, and tie it to future learning. To demonstrate the importance of using the *Give Me Five: Stop and Listen* strategy, use the A/B pair discussion technique (see page 14). Have one student tell why it is important to be prepared to listen. Have the other student describe other classroom or home situations when appropriate listening body language is beneficial. Have all adults use the "give me five" signal throughout the day as a way to gain students' attention (e.g., while lining up for recess or lunch, when giving instructions, when giving important information pertaining to assignments and/or homework). In the next lesson, students will have an opportunity to listen actively for extended periods of time.

CAREful LISTENING (PART I)

GOAL

To improve listening skills

BACKGROUND INFORMATION

Please note the partner book in the *Language Strategies* series, *Language Strategies for Children: Keys to Classroom Success*, uses CARE as an acronym in its *Listening* lesson: *C*oncentrating on the listening job, *A*lerting the brain when key words and phrases signal the need to listen, *R*epeating the important information silently, and *E*valuating the information to ensure understanding. The CARE strategy has been modified in *Language Strategies for Little Ones* to make it an age-appropriate strategy: You have to care to use CAREful listening. The word *care* is capitalized only as a way to bridge the two complementary books.

The main focus of this lesson is to provide students with an opportunity to listen actively for extended periods of time with the addition of distractors. The distractors in these lessons are visual (pictures), physical (props), and environmental (neighbors with props, a variety of speakers, frequent group responses, and sound effects). The distractions in Part I are presented during an activity that has students listen for erroneous information that does not match the visual information presented. By using CAREful listening, the students should ignore distractions and ask for clarification when needed. Students can be reminded of this by saying, "You need to care to use CAREful listening."

In Part I, the educator will use art prints (i.e., poster-sized works of well-known artists [e.g., Frederic Remington and Winslow Homer]), which are available through a number of sources, such as school or public libraries, art teachers, or CD-ROM collections. Because of the variety of art prints available, the educator can choose prints to fit a theme and to reinforce age-appropriate concepts and curriculum while practicing listening skills. For example, the action-filled painting *Dismounted*, by Frederic Remington, can be used as a tie-in to geography, or Winslow Homer's painting *Snap the Whip* can be used to compare an old-fashioned school to one in modern times.

HINT

Contrasting action pictures with more peaceful prints creates an interesting flow to the lesson.

OBJECTIVES

1. Listen actively for specific information.
2. Recognize the need for clarification.
3. Request clarification appropriately.

MATERIALS

1. Einstein character (Recommended but not necessary; see page 12.)
2. *Be a CAREful Listener* graphic (See page 38; duplicate and enlarge the graphic, color it, mount it onto colorful construction paper or poster board, and laminate it for durability, if desired.)
3. Assorted art prints

INTRODUCTION

Tie-in to Prior Learning

Have Einstein say:

> *Last week we practiced being active listeners by getting into our listening position whenever we saw or heard "Give me five." Who remembers our five rules?* (eyes on the speaker, mouth quiet, body still, ears listening, and hands free) *What other part of your body has to be working in order for you to listen?* (your brain) *Let's see how quickly you can show me that you're ready to listen and learn!*

Focus/Relevancy

Have Einstein tell the students about a mistake Professor Green made by calling him the wrong name. Have Einstein ask the students if their teacher ever makes a mistake by calling a student the wrong name or by giving the wrong directions. Have the students think about what they should say. Ask them if it would sound very nice if they said to their teacher (read these responses in a sarcastic or rude voice), "You called me by the wrong name!" or "That's not my name!"Allow a few minutes for discussion. Tell the students that today they are going to learn a polite way to ask for *clarification*. Say:

> *This special word means "something that you ask for when what you heard is not clear or you don't understand." Let's practice saying this word together by clapping out all the sounds using a golf clap.*

(Use the golf clap [see page 12] to clap out the syllables while saying the word *clar/i/fi/ca/tion* together.) Continue:

> *If I said, "I'm so glad that you could come to school tonight," you would probably need clarification, because my statement didn't make sense.*

Ask the students why this response is not very clear. Prompt the students in a discussion to determine that it is morning, or daytime, not night. Practice the polite way to ask for clarification by saying, "Excuse me, but I don't understand why you said 'come to school *tonight*.'"

HINT

It is helpful to write on the board as a visual prompt the polite beginning to any request for clarification (e.g., "Excuse me, but…").

LESSON ACTIVITIES

1. Show the *Be a CAREful Listener* poster. Point out that Einstein is being a CAREful listener; he is asking for clarification because he needs more information or because he heard a mistake. Emphasize that students need to care to use CAREful listening.

2. Tell students that they are going to practice being CAREful listeners by trying to catch when you give information that does not make sense or that is wrong. Explain that you will describe a number of art prints and will purposely say things that are wrong. Tell students to signal whenever they hear a "mistake" and to politely ask for clarification then.

   HINT

   Purposefully do not tell the students how to signal. Ask the students if they need any clarification of the instructions. If there is no response, ask who knows how to signal. The educator may tell them to signal by touching their nose, giving the thumbs-up signal, raising their hand, etc. Students will then be called upon to politely ask for clarification.

   The following scripts have been used by the authors as examples. Choose from a variety of interesting prints to practice CAREful listening. (The italicized information is the script. The words/phrases within the parentheses describe what is actually seen in the painting.) After you make a "mistake" and students have signaled and politely asked for clarification, take the opportunity to discuss the curricular connections that can be made (e.g., discussing desert versus forest).

   - Artist: Frederic Remington, *Dismounted—The 4th Troopers Moving*, 1890

     This painting by Frederic Remmington is full of action! The green grass of the forest looks cool and peaceful (hot, dusty desert, noisy). *The horses are walking slowing* (galloping). *One soldier has three black* (white, black, and brown) *horses tied together, while the other soldiers are all riding their own horses* (some soldiers are lying down or shooting at an enemy).

   - Artist: Horace Pippin, *Victorian Interior*, 1946

     This is a painting by the artist Horace Pippin. He wanted to paint a picture of a pretty bedroom (a living room or den; discuss appropriate furniture for various locations). *There is a big, oval table between two red* (green) *chairs. There are two paintings on the walls. The small* (large) *table has a bouquet of flowers on it. The chair on the right* (left) *has a lace decoration in the shape of a triangle, and the chair on the left* (right) *has a square lace decoration. The person who lived in this house must have liked to read books and crochet using blue* (white) *yarn.*

- Artist: Winslow Homer, *Snap the Whip,* 1872

  This painting shows boys playing Nintendo in a bustling city (not playing, small schoolhouse, Nintendo not yet invented; discuss modern times versus historical times). *The schoolhouse is a small, red, one-room building. Since the boys are all wearing their hats and shoes, they are ready for gym class* (Most of the boys are wearing hats but not shoes). *What a beautiful, clear* (cloudy), *sunny day to play outside!*

- Artist: Winslow Homer, *Breezing Up,* 1876

  One afternoon a group of friends decided to go fishing, so they found Ol' Fisherman Bob. He was wearing a straw (felt) *fishing hat and a bright blue* (red) *shirt. He agreed to take them out in his shiny new motorboat* (sailboat). *The boys climbed aboard, put on their orange life jackets* (no life jackets) *and settled into their seats. Bob and the four boys set sail. The ocean was as calm and still as a sheet of glass* (waves) *and there were no clouds in the blue sky* (cloudy). *The boys fished all afternoon, but with no luck. They came home empty-handed* (fish in the boat).

3. Use this activity for additional practice. Students enjoy "surprising" visitors.

   Let's surprise our visitors by showing what we have learned today. When someone new comes into the room, I will say something that doesn't make sense. I want everyone to use a whisper voice to politely ask for clarification. This shows that you care about being CAREful listeners.

CLOSURE

Summarize the lesson, repeat its relevance to students, and tie it to future learning. Remind the students that they can practice this new skill at school and at home, and that their teachers and parents will appreciate their CAREful listening and good manners when questioning something that doesn't make sense. In the next lesson, students will practice what to do when noisy distractions make listening difficult.

Be A CAREful LISTENER
Bzzzz
Blah! Blah!
"Excuse me, but..."
oooh!

CAREful LISTENING (PART II)

GOAL

To improve listening skills

BACKGROUND INFORMATION

The main focus of this lesson is to provide students with an opportunity to listen actively for extended periods of time with the addition of distractors. The distractors in these lessons are visual (pictures), physical (props), and environmental (neighbors with props, a variety of speakers, frequent group responses, and sound effects). The distractions in Part II are presented during an activity that has students listen for their cues to make various sound effects while manipulating props and performing a story as it is recorded on tape. By using CAREful listening, students should ignore distractions and ask for clarification when needed. Students can be reminded of this by saying, "You need to care to use CAREful listening."

OBJECTIVES

1. Listen actively for specific information.
2. Recognize the need for clarification.
3. Request clarification appropriately.
4. Identify potential interfering noises or distractions.

MATERIALS

1. Einstein character (Recommended but not necessary; see page 12.)
2. *Be a CAREful Listener* poster (Created earlier)
3. *Too Much Noise* (1992), by Ann McGovern, illustrated by Simms Taback (This book was chosen because of the many sound effect words and the numerous opportunities for children to participate.)
4. Popsicle stick animal puppets (See page 42; duplicate, cut out, and glue them onto popsicle sticks. Make enough of the characters for every child to have a part. Five of each should cover most class sizes.)
5. Audio or video recording equipment

INTRODUCTION

Tie-in to Prior Learning

Have Einstein remind the students that in the last lesson, they practiced being CAREful listeners by learning what to do when they heard a mistake or when the information did not make sense. Have a student model asking for clarification. Review the idea that students must care to use CAREful listening.

Focus/Relevancy

Have Einstein say:

Today we are going to be performing our own special story. We will practice our brand-new skill of being CAREful listeners.

LESSON ACTIVITIES

1. Show the *Be a CAREful Listener* poster, and discuss the distractions that are going on in the graphic (i.e., a fly buzzing around, frogs playing with props and talking). Explain how Einstein can solve his problem by keeping his brain focused on his work and by ignoring the distractions. Tell the students that they will practice being CAREful listeners today by concentrating with their ears and brain and by ignoring lots of distractions like Einstein did.

2. Show the students the book *Too Much Noise* and highlight the author and the illustrator. Explain that in this story, there is a character who tries to solve a problem by asking a wise, old man for help. Ask the students what the word *wise* means. Tell the students that they will decide after listening to the story whether the man really is wise.

   Explain to the students that they will each be given a special prop to use in the performance of the story. Remind them of how Einstein solved his distraction problems; show the *Be a CAREful Listener* poster once again.

   Demonstrate the use of the popsicle stick animal puppets by showing that when a sound is mentioned in the story, the listener should raise that particular puppet and make the sound (e.g., when the teacher reads "the cow mooed," the students who have a cow stick puppet should raise their picture and make mooing noises).

   Before passing out the puppets, stress to the students that they are being challenged to keep their prop (puppet) on the floor or on their desk in front of them until it is their turn to participate in the story. Explain that they will have a chance to demonstrate their sound effect before the story begins. To make certain that each student understands his or her respective role, have the students lift up their puppet and make the appropriate sound as the teacher names it (e.g., the cow moos or the donkey hee-haws). Use the "give me five" signal to indicate when everyone should be quiet and listen for the next animal.

HINT

Have the entire class make the household sounds, such as the floor creaking, bed squeaking, kettle whistling, and leaves swishing. This allows the students to stay more engaged when having to listen for an extended period of time.

3. Remind students that their performance is going to be recorded, so they will need to use the *CAREful Listening* strategy and wait silently for their part to come. Tell them that the audiotape (or videotape) will pick up *all* the sounds in the room and that they do not want to put distracting noises in their recording.

   Ask the students if anyone needs clarification. Answer any questions before beginning to record.

   Tape-record the performance. Make sure that the tape recorder is placed where it can pick up all sounds. Add a fun, professional recording atmosphere by saying:

   > *Quiet on the set! 5...4...3...2...1... Presenting* Too Much Noise, *starring (Mrs. MacCarthy's kindergarten class).*

   Begin reading and continue until the story is completed. Collect the props while rewinding the tape.

4. Have the class listen to and/or watch their performance and evaluate the accuracy of their sound effects. Ask the students if there were many distracting sounds:

   > *Did it take a lot of effort to concentrate for a performance? What helped you concentrate despite all the distractions? Did you listen carefully and ignore the distractions like Einstein did?*

   Using the A/B pair discussion technique (see page 14), have students share ways to stay focused (e.g., keeping their prop on the floor until it is their turn or ignoring the other sounds in order to follow along with the narrator).

CLOSURE

Summarize the lesson, repeat its relevance to students, and tie it to future learning. Remind the students that they have been practicing being CAREful listeners by ignoring distractions and listening with their ears and their brain. In the next lesson, the students will practice other ways to ask for information.

CLARIFYING WITH QUESTION WORDS (PART I)

GOAL

To improve listening during question-answer exchanges

BACKGROUND INFORMATION

The main purpose of this lesson is to teach the concept of asking a question, rather than telling information, and to emphasize CAREfully listening to the answer. Students' difficulty with knowing the difference between asking and telling is most apparent when the educator says, "Do you have any questions?" and students respond by making a comment.

OBJECTIVES

1. Recognize the difference between asking and telling.
2. Recognize question words and the question mark symbol.
3. Ask questions to gain information.
4. Listen carefully to answers to questions.

MATERIALS

1. Einstein character (Recommended but not necessary; see page 12.)
2. Social application story: *Use Your Question Words!* (See pages 45–53; also see page 7.)
3. Question word graphics (See pages 54–59; duplicate and enlarge the graphics, color them, mount them onto colorful construction paper or poster board, and laminate them for durability, if desired.)

INTRODUCTION

Tie-in to Prior Learning

Have Einstein remind the students that in the last lesson, they practiced being CAREful listeners by ignoring distractions while recording a story. They had to work hard to keep their brain focused on their listening job.

Focus/Relevancy

Say to the students:

> *Have you ever wondered something? Maybe you've wondered what Mom is cooking for dinner or which presents you'll get for your birthday. When we want to find out information, we can*

use special words that help us gather information. In today's lesson, Einstein is going to learn to use these special words.

Show the cover of the social application story *Use Your Question Words!* Explain that Einstein will learn how using question words is an important tool for gathering information. Discuss situations where the students may want to gather information (e.g., learning about animals, new places to visit, or famous people) and how they need to listen to the answers they get.

LESSON ACTIVITIES

1. Read the social application story. The story centers around a special visitor that is coming to the pond. Note that when Professor Green asks for questions the student frogs might have about the visitor, Einstein raises his hand and tells about an event, rather than asking for or gathering information. Emphasize Professor Green's comment as it relates to the difference between asking and telling. Using the question words posters, have Einstein practice using the question words *what, who, where, when, why,* and *how*. Use the frog puppet to model question word use (e.g., on the "What" page, Einstein may ask, "*What* do you wear when it is cold out?" or "*What* can you eat as a treat?"). Following each question, allow time for students to raise their hand and respond. Others may signal with their golf clap (see page 12) if they agree. Point out that it takes CAREful listening to questions to know how to answer.

2. Ask the students to think of things they would like to know about Einstein. Model some examples, "Hmmm… I wonder what Einstein likes to eat… I'll ASK! Einstein, what do you like to eat?" (Make the frog puppet respond appropriately.) "Hmmm… I wonder who is in Einstein's family… I'll ASK! Einstein, who is in your family?" Other ideas might be where his pond is, what he likes to do in his spare time, or how he learned to swim. Call on students or student pairs to practice using their question words to gather information about Einstein. The students are extremely motivated by this activity and enjoy asking Einstein questions. Have Einstein give any appropriate answers. Emphasize CAREfully listening to the answers. "Quiz" students about Einstein's answers to determine how well they listened after asking their questions.

CLOSURE

Summarize the lesson, repeat its relevance to students, and tie it to future learning. Remind the students that they can practice this new skill by using question words whenever they wonder about something. In Part II of this lesson, students will use question words to help them gather information about a special visitor to their classroom!

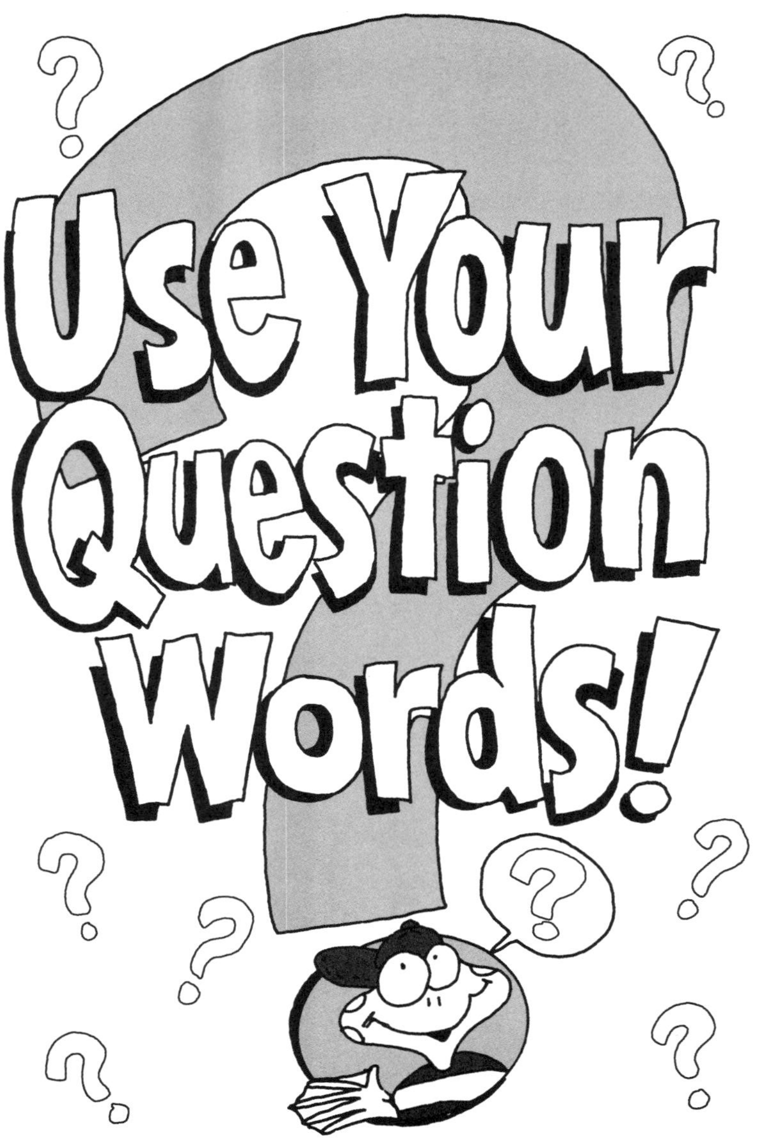

A special visitor is coming to our pond!

Can you gather facts to reveal the visitor's identity?

When you gather information, you ask a question.

What
would you
like to know
about our
Special
Visitor?

2

"We had a special visit from my grandparents!"

Is Einstein asking or telling?

He needs to find out information about the visitor.

3

4

Hmmm...
I wonder where it lives...

I'll ask!

"Where does our visitor live?"

5

"It lives on tree leaves
and branches."

6

Hmmm...
I wonder what it eats...

I'll ask!

"What does our
visitor eat?"

7

Professor Green answers...

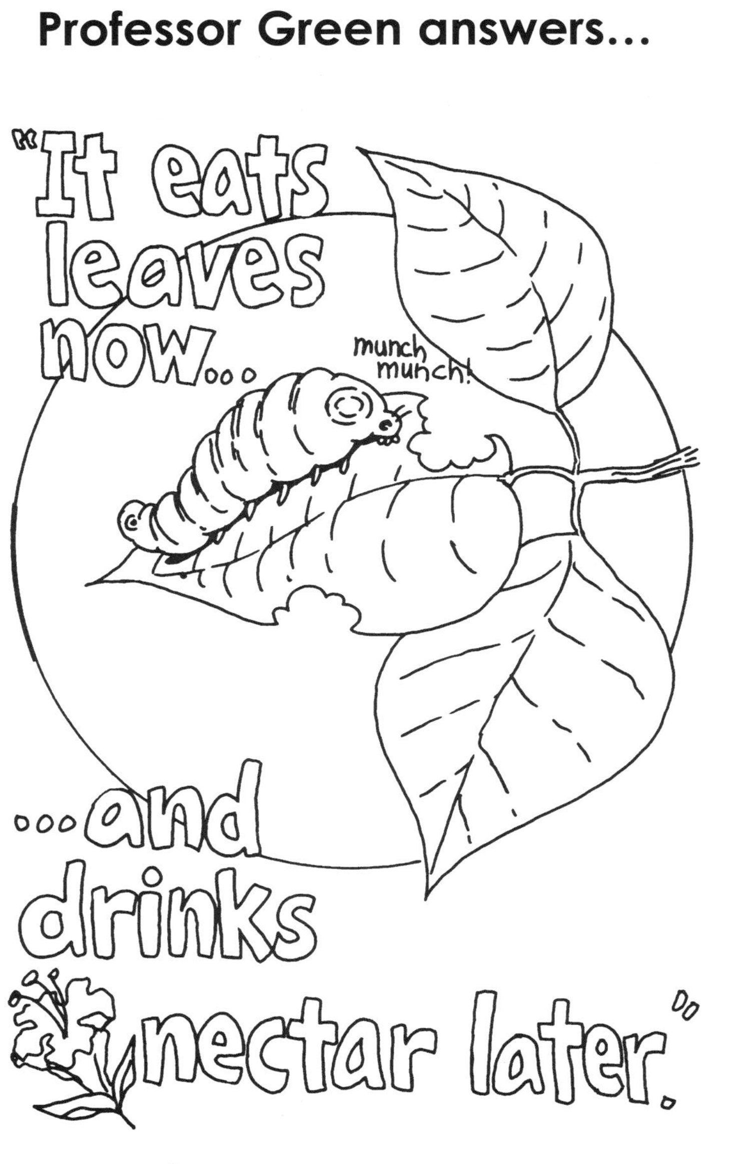

8

Hmmm...
I wonder how it will get here...

I'll ask!

"How will our visitor get to the pond?"

9

"It will fly!"

10

Hmmm...
I wonder when it will be here...

I'll ask!

"When will our
visitor come?"

11

"It will come in spring."

12

Hmmm...
I wonder why it will
take so long...
I'll ask!

"Why will it take so
long to
get
here?"

13

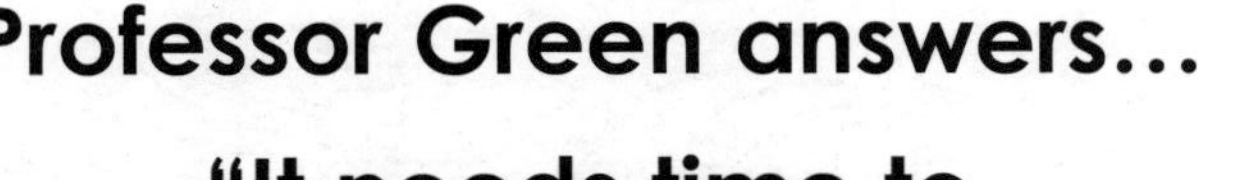

Professor Green answers...

"It needs time to change and grow!"

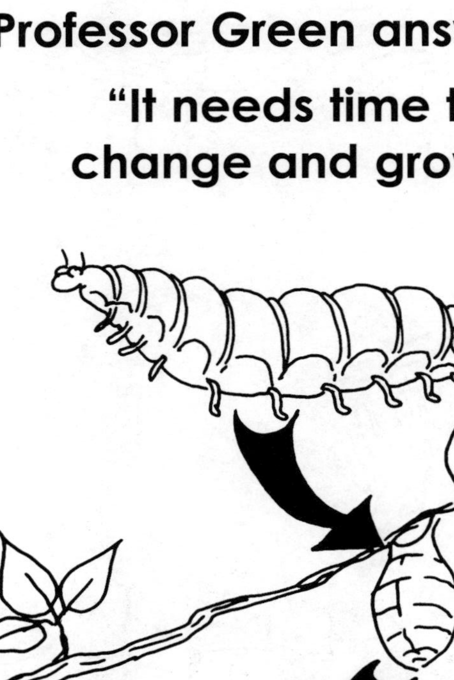

14

Hmmm...

I wonder...

"Who is it?"

15

Professor Green answers…
“It’s Miss Butterfly!”
16

What?

Who?

Where?

January
S M T W T F S
1 2 3 4 5 6 7
8 9 10 11 12 13 14
15 16 17 18 19 20 21
22 23 24 25 26 27 28
29 30 31
When?
XII
IX
III
VI

Why?
For You!

Seeds
HOW?
Seeds

CLARIFYING WITH QUESTION WORDS (PART II)

GOAL

To improve listening during question-answer exchanges

BACKGROUND INFORMATION

The main purpose of this lesson is to let students practice using question words to gather information about a special visitor and to emphasize CAREfully listening to the answers. These questions will be presented in the form of an interview.

OBJECTIVES

1. Recognize the difference between asking and telling.
2. Recognize question words and the question mark symbol.
3. Ask questions to gain information.
4. Listen carefully to answers to questions.

MATERIALS

1. Einstein character (Recommended but not necessary; see page 12.)
2. Social application story: *Use Your Question Words!* (See pages 45–53; also see page 7.)
3. *Use Your Question Words!* graphic (See page 62; duplicate and enlarge the graphic, color it, mount it onto colorful construction paper or poster board, and laminate it for durability, if desired.)
4. *Interview Chart* (See page 63; duplicate and enlarge the chart, color it, mount it onto colorful construction paper or poster board, and laminate it for durability, if desired.)
5. A special visitor to be interviewed by the students (e.g., the principal, nurse, librarian, music teacher, or someone from the community).
6. *An Interview* homework page (See page 64.)

INTRODUCTION

Tie-in to Prior Learning

Have Einstein remind the students that in the last lesson, he practiced using his question words to gather information about a special visitor who was coming to his pond. Review the question words and write them on the board. Remind students they also listened CAREfully to answers.

Focus/Relevancy

Continue by having Einstein lead the students in a discussion. Have the students raise their hand if they have ever seen Kermit the Frog on the show *Sesame Street*. Ask the students if they have ever seen

Kermit find out information about special visitors, such as Goldilocks, on his show by conducting an interview (use the golf clap to clap out the syllables *in/ter/view*). Demonstrate how Kermit might use his microphone while asking his special guest different questions (e.g., "How did you get inside the three bears' house?" "Was the baby bear's porridge really the best?"). Explain that they will be using question words to gather information about a special visitor to their classroom.

LESSON ACTIVITIES

1. Explain that an interview is a way to find out interesting facts or information about someone important or fascinating. It is a way to learn about different people. Show the *Use Your Question Words!* poster, and review the question words that were introduced in the *Use Your Question Words!* social application story from Part I. Model an interview with a student.

2. Have the students practice "reading" the *Interview Chart* together. Announce who the special visitor is whom they will be interviewing. Brainstorm questions that could be asked. Practice asking them. Bring in the special visitor, and have students ask him or her their interview questions. Remind them to listen CAREfully to the answers.

   HINT
   In a large group setting, so that everyone has an opportunity to participate, you may want to have the students seated in five rows or groups so that each row/group can practice asking the guest a specific question from the chart.

3. To provide an opportunity for continued practice with asking questions, introduce the *An Interview* homework page. Have pairs of students come to the front of the class and demonstrate asking questions from the page and telling about themselves. Take a few minutes for each person to have a turn.

4. Tell the students that they need to interview someone in their family. Explain that they will be finding out something new and interesting about their mom or dad or other important person at home. They will need to be CAREful listeners to get the information.

   HINT
   Having the students return this homework for a special stamp or sticker increases the likelihood the assignment will be returned.

CLOSURE

Summarize the lesson, repeat its relevance to students, and tie it to future learning. Tell the students that they can practice this new skill by taking *An Interview* home to interview one or more members of their family. In the next lesson, the students will use their clarification skills to help them give and follow directions.

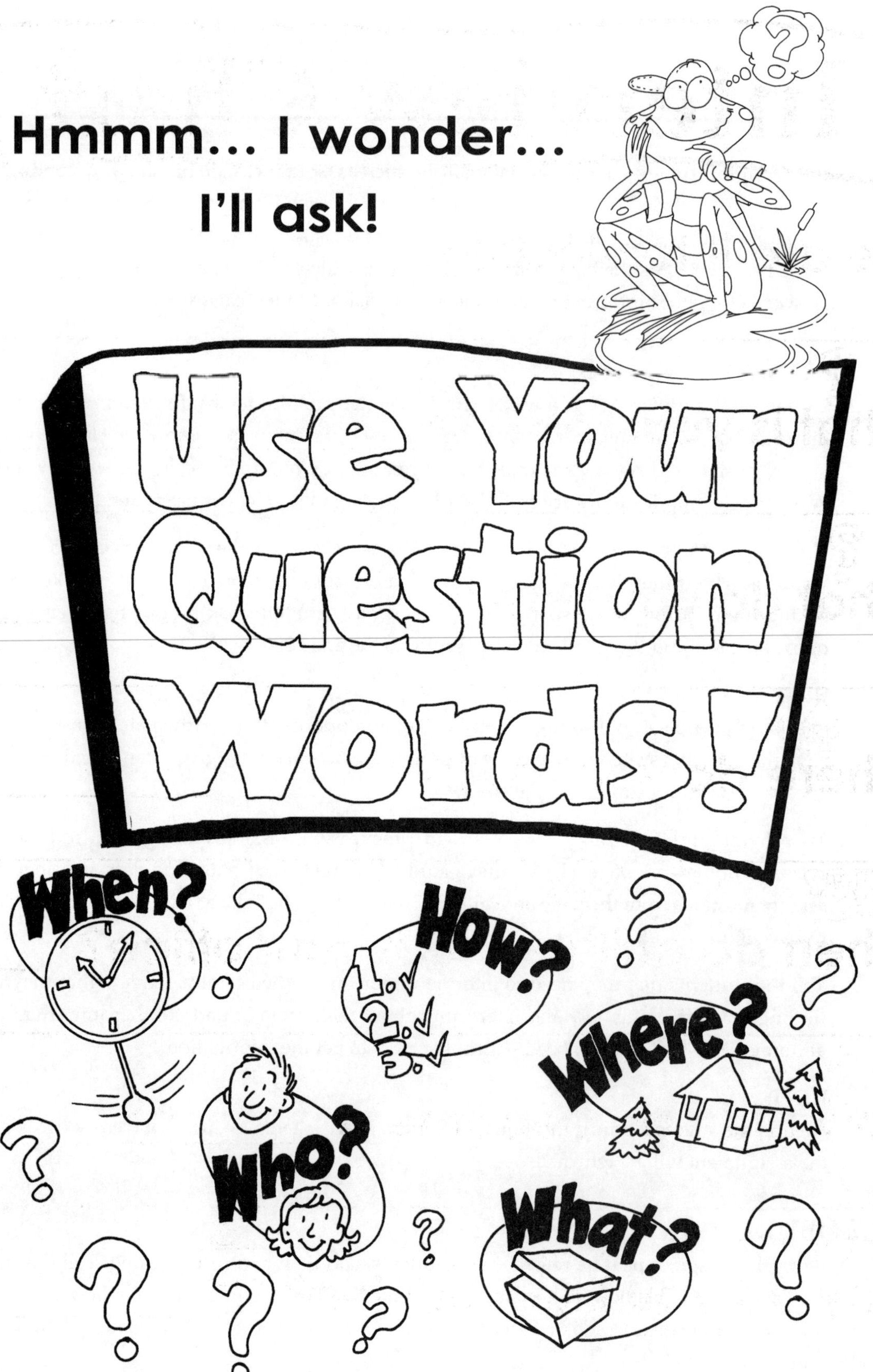
Hmmm... I wonder...
I'll ask!
Use Your Question Words!
When?
How?
1.
2.
3.
Where?
Who?
What?

Interview Chart

We are interviewing:

____

What is your job? ________________________

____

What do you do? ________________________

____

Where do you work? ____________________

____

When do children visit your office? ____

____

How did you become a ______________ **?**

____

Why do you like your job? ____________

____

An Interview

We use our question words to gather information.

My name: ______________________________

I am interviewing: ______________________

What is your favorite food? ___________

____

Where were you born? _________________

____

When is your birthday? _______________

____

Who is your hero? ______________________

____

Why? _____________________________________

HIT THE BULL'S-EYE: GIVING AND FOLLOWING DIRECTIONS

GOAL

To improve comprehension while listening to directions

BACKGROUND INFORMATION

The main focus of this lesson is to evaluate given information during listening situations. This lesson encourages the student to ask the questions Does it make sense? Do I have enough information? Is it a reasonable request?

OBJECTIVES

1. Review what the word *clarification* means.
2. Know when and how to ask for clarification when given insufficient directions or information.
3. Use age-appropriate vocabulary for basic concepts when giving clear directions.

MATERIALS

1. Einstein character (Recommended but not necessary; see page 12.)
2. *Use Your Question Words!* poster (Created earlier)
3. *Hit the Bull's-Eye* graphic (See page 68; duplicate and enlarge the graphic, color it, mount it onto colorful construction paper or poster board, and laminate it for durability, if desired.)
4. Basic construction paper shapes that make a house (i.e., a large square frame, triangle roof, rectangle door, small square window)
5. Pond scene with items to be placed on the picture (Duplicate the scene, color it, and laminate it for durability [see page 69]. Duplicate, color, cut out, and laminate the smaller items [see pages 70–71].)

NOTE: For identical items, be sure to make them different colors (e.g., one orange butterfly, one purple butterfly).

HINT

If a magnetic chalkboard is available, add magnetic strips to the pond scene and to the smaller individual pieces to allow everyone to see and to learn along with the students who are giving and following the directions. Otherwise, the pieces will need to be taped to the board so that everyone can see.

INTRODUCTION

Tie-in to Prior Learning

Have Einstein remind students that in the last lesson, the students practiced asking questions and telling information. Review the question words from the last lesson using the *Use Your Question Words!* poster. Have Einstein ask who remembers the special word that means "something that you ask for when you politely ask for more information when a message is not clear" (i.e., *clarification*). Practice saying this word together by golf clapping it out: *clar/i/fi/ca/tion*.

Focus/Relevancy

Continue to use the Einstein character as the instructor, or set him aside until you wish to incorporate the puppet or character as the instructor again. To set up a situation where the directions are unclear and the students will need clarification, have students follow imprecise directions using the simple shapes. First ask the students to name the different shapes (i.e., a large square, a triangle, a rectangle, and a small square). Tell a student, "Put the square on the board." If the student asks for clarification, compliment him or her on CAREful listening and thinking, since there were two different squares to choose from. If the student does not ask for more information, continue to give imprecise directions, such as, "Put the triangle on the square. Put the rectangle on the square. Put the square on." Now ask the students if these shapes look like a house. Choose a student to give directions for arranging the shapes to look like a house. Encourage them to use question words when more information is needed, and emphasize the use of specific direction words or phrases (e.g., *above, below, in the middle, on the left/right*) to make the message clear.

LESSON ACTIVITIES

1. Show the *Hit the Bull's-Eye* poster. Point out the Einstein character in the poster and how by using clear, specific directions, he is able to hit the bull's-eye and "build the house" with his words. Relate the poster to the imprecise directions that were given during the *focus/relevancy* activity (e.g., "Put the square on the board" was not specific, because it did not tell which square to choose, or "Put the triangle on the square" was not a precise direction, so clarification was needed).

   Say to the students:

   When directions are clear and specific, we can hit the bull's-eye every time.

2. To prepare for this activity, highlight basic concepts by placing different items on the pond scene to demonstrate the concepts of beside, next to, right, left, over, under, in, on, in front of,

behind, etc. Explain how the use of specific vocabulary can make directions clearer. Return to the example of "Put the triangle on the square." Ask the students if they would know exactly what to do. (Demonstrate the potential confusion by placing the triangle in the middle of the square.) Next tell the students how to make the directions clearer. Say, "Put the triangle above the large square so that the side of it touches the top side of the square" (demonstrate appropriate placement).

HINT
Remind the students that you will only call on quiet students with their hand raised. The use of the golf clap or thumbs-up signal to show that students have the same answer is a way to let a larger number of students participate.

3. Tell the students that they will practice giving and following directions using a special picture of Einstein's pond. Attach the pond scene to the board, and show all the different items that Einstein might find around his home. Hold up the items in contrasting pairs, and let students tell how the pictures are different (e.g., a big tree and a little tree, an orange butterfly and a purple butterfly).

   Choose one student at a time to tell where to place an object on the picture. Place the object exactly as stated by the student. Use the child's "mistakes" to show the need for clarification when imprecise directions are given (e.g., "Is the tree above the pond? On the left or right side? Near the flower?").

   HINT
   When the pond scene is too full, or when all the objects have been used, clear the board and start again. Continue the activity until all students have had an opportunity to give a direction. Alternatively, duplicate pond scenes and items for pairs of students to use simultaneously.

CLOSURE

Summarize the lesson, review its relevance to students, and tie it to future learning. Review once more the important strategies that were stressed within this lesson (i.e., using specific vocabulary when giving directions and asking for clarification when information is unclear). Remind students that these will be useful skills in the classroom if they want to hit the bull's-eye like Einstein did. In the next lesson, students will review all the strategies taught in Unit One.

HIT THE BULL'S-EYE!
DOES IT MAKE SENSE?
DO I NEED MORE INFORMATION?

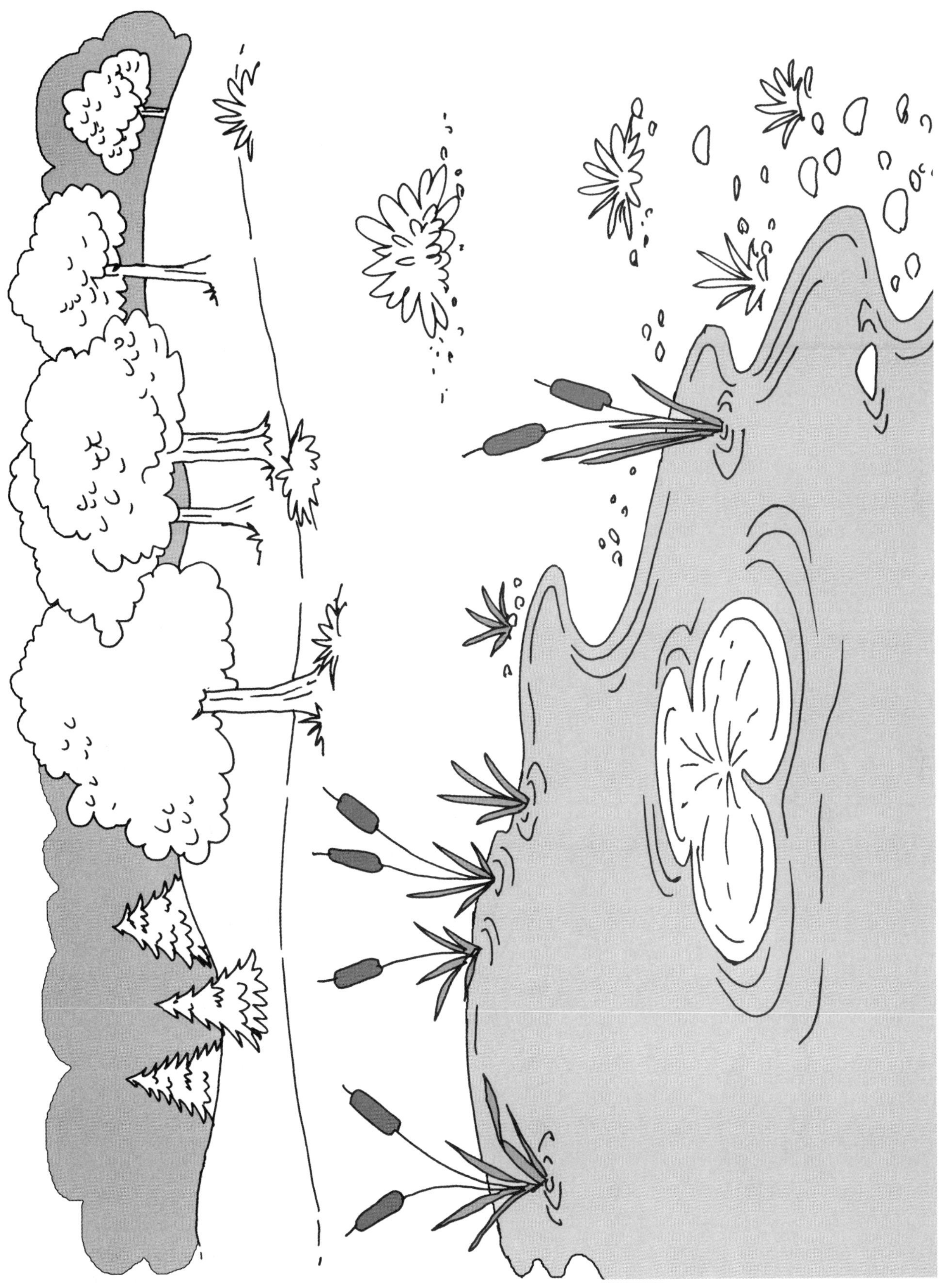

STRATEGY REVIEW LESSON 1

GOAL

To reinforce and review the strategies for listening and language comprehension

BACKGROUND INFORMATION

The main focus of this lesson is to review the listening strategies: *Give Me Five, CAREful Listening, Clarifying with Question Words,* and *Hit the Bull's-Eye.* A review lesson is provided after several strategies have been taught. In addition, the students take home the *Homework Activity* pages and *Communication Skills Newsletter No. 1* to encourage family involvement and understanding of the language skills.

OBJECTIVES

1. Review and practice the major components of the *Give Me Five, CAREful Listening, Clarifying with Question Words,* and *Hit the Bull's-Eye* strategies.
2. Complete the application activities.
3. Share strategy information with family members.

MATERIALS

1. Einstein character (Recommended but not necessary; see page 12.)
2. *Give Me Five* poster (Created earlier)
3. *Be a CAREful Listener* poster (Created earlier)
4. *Use Your Question Words!* poster (Created earlier)
5. *Hit the Bull's-Eye* poster (Created earlier)
6. *Homework Activity* pages (See pages 74–78; duplicate for each student.)
7. *Skills Checklist* (See page 79; duplicate and enlarge the checklist, color it, mount it onto colorful construction paper or poster board, and laminate it, if desired.)
8. *Communication Skills Newsletter No. 1* (See pages 80–81; duplicate for each student.)

INTRODUCTION

Tie-in to Prior Learning

Einstein can remind the students that they have been learning many important skills to help them become better listeners. Display and briefly review the posters and strategies for these lessons.

Focus/Relevancy

Have Einstein ask the students to show with a thumbs-up signal if they have ever had to do homework or if they have a brother or sister who has to do homework. He can tell them that they are going to have a special homework assignment, to be worked on with an older family member. Tell the students that their families will be really impressed when they hear how much they have learned!

LESSON ACTIVITIES

1. Briefly show the students the *Homework Activity* pages and display the posters *(Give Me Five, Be a CAREful Listener, Use Your Question Words!*, and *Hit the Bull's-Eye*).
2. Review each skill by having Einstein select several students to model it for the class or by having the entire class give choral responses to his review questions from the *Homework Activity* pages (e.g., Have the students state and demonstrate the *Give Me Five* listening body language. Have the students practice polite requests for clarification while being CAREful listeners by saying together, "Excuse me, but...").
3. Display the *Skills Checklist.* Review the key components of a lesson by looking at the poster and by practicing some items from the *Homework Activity* pages. Place or have students place a checkmark on the line beside each skill as the review is completed.
4. Show the students *Communication Skills Newsletter No. 1.* Explain that even their parents have homework. The newsletter describes the activities that they have been doing in class.
5. Hand out the *Homework Activity* pages and *Communication Skills Newsletter No. 1* for the students to take home, or place them in envelopes for students to take home.

CLOSURE

Summarize the lesson, review its relevance to students, and tie it to future learning. Have Einstein encourage the students to share their *Homework Activity* pages and *Communication Skills Newsletter No. 1* with someone special at home. Explain that after they have completed the homework, they should have their parent or caregiver sign and date in the appropriate space and return it for a reward (e.g., a sticker or points on a homework chart). In the next lesson, students will begin the oral expression lessons by using precise descriptions.

Homework Activity

Name: ______________________________

1. When giving directions or important information to your child, be sure that you have your child's full attention. (Remind them of the *Give Me Five: Stop and Listen* strategy: eyes on the speaker, mouth quiet, body still, ears listening, and hands free).
2. Have your child remember two or three items from your grocery list. Have him or her repeat the list aloud.
3. Read a familiar story, change the wording, and see if your child catches the "mistake." Practice using polite clarification (e.g., "Excuse me, but did you mean…").
4. Give your child two or three jobs to do (e.g., sorting the silverware, picking up dirty clothes and bringing them to the laundry room, or helping put groceries away). Have your child repeat the directions *before* starting the task.
5. Encourage your child to ask questions when he or she doesn't understand what to do. If your child only asks a certain type of question (e.g., "What is…?"), you might need to model or emphasize *who, where, when, why,* or *how* questions.
6. Play a game with your child in which you take turns giving clear, specific directions to find a certain object. For example, "Find the blue cup that is in the kitchen on the counter next to the stove" or "Find the stuffed rabbit that is in the living room behind the couch."

The ability to communicate is one of our most valuable tools, and I hope these activity ideas will be a helpful tool for you and your child. Please sign below to indicate you have done one or more of these activities with your child.

Family Member: ______________________________ Date: ____________________

Homework Activity

Name: ______________________________

Dear Family,

1. Have your child "teach" you the five important things to do when giving your full attention and listening. (HINT: Use the pictures on each finger for a clue!)
2. Listen to the sounds you hear in your house. If you concentrate, can you hear sounds from outside?
3. Have your child listen for one thing to remember from your grocery list. Have him or her remind you of this item once you get into the store.

Family Member: ______________________ Date: ______________

Homework Activity

Name: ____

Dear Family,

1. Practice CAREful listening and politely requesting clar-i-fi-ca-tion by having your child say "Excuse me, but…" after you read the following:

   a. The laundry is in the oven.

   b. We need to cut the lawn mower.

2. Read a familiar story. Make a "mistake" while reading or looking at the pictures. Your child can practice requesting clarification when they catch your "mistake"!

Family Member: ______________________________ Date: ____________________

Homework Activity

We use our question words to gather information. Take turns asking and answering questions with someone at home. Listen CAREfully to the answers.

My name: ______________________________

I am interviewing: ______________________

What is your favorite sport? __________

____

Where do you like to go for fun? ____

____

When do you wake up? ______________

____

Who is your favorite TV character? __

____

Why? ___________________________________

Family Member: ______________________ Date: ______________

Homework Activity

Name: ______________________________

Create a pond scene. Cut along the dotted lines to separate items. Be spe-ci-fic when telling where you want them placed. (HINT: Use your "where" words—*on, over, under, next to*). Play with a partner!

Family Member: ______________________ Date: ______________

Skills Checklist

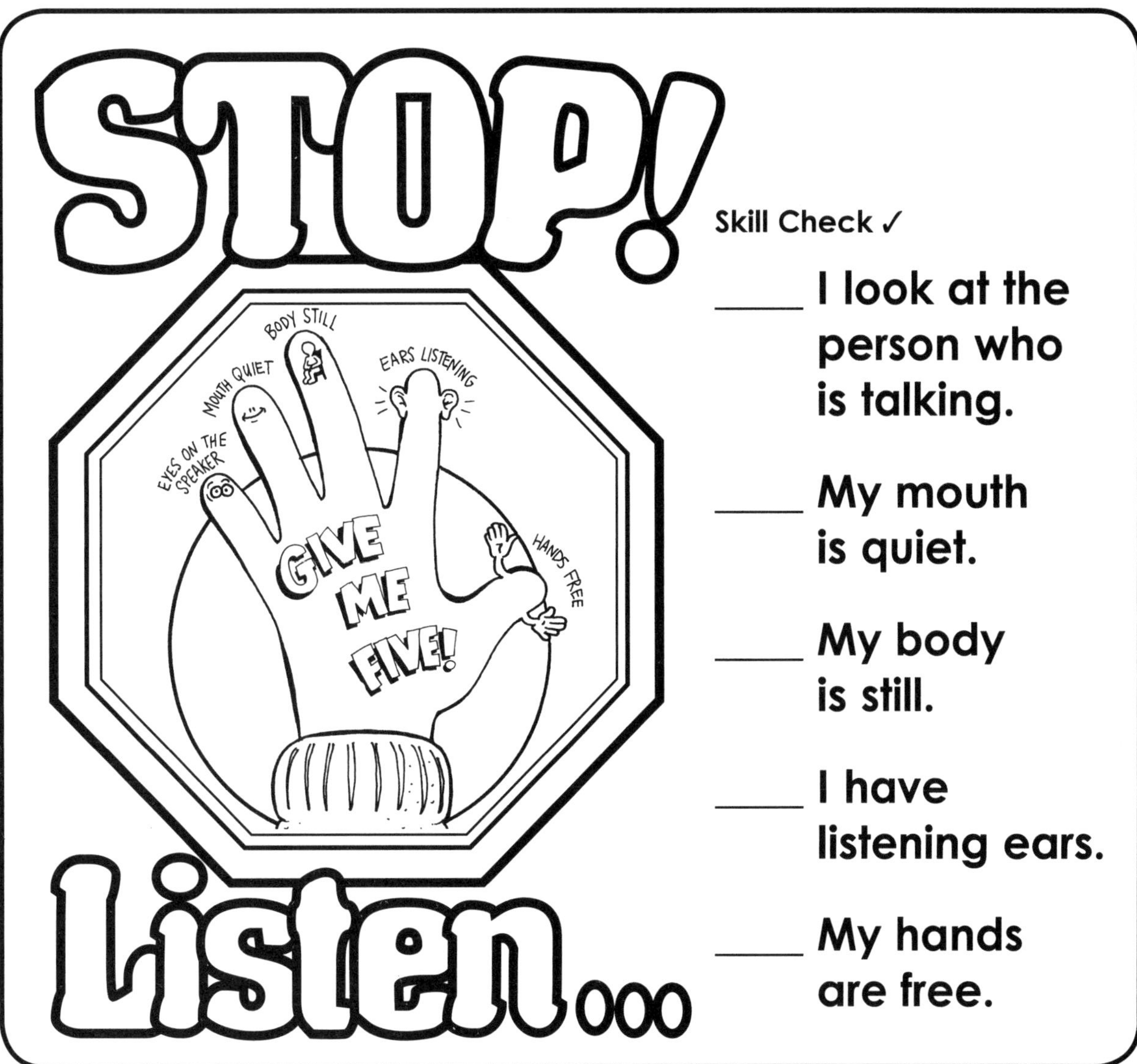

Skill Check ✓

____ I look at the person who is talking.

____ My mouth is quiet.

____ My body is still.

____ I have listening ears.

____ My hands are free.

When something doesn't make sense...

I use my polite words to

ASK for CLAR•I•FI•CA•TION

(Clap it out!)

Communication Skills Newsletter

No. 1

Welcome to Our Newsletter!

Your child has been enjoying a communication skills program that goes along with the classroom language arts program for kindergarten and first grade. You will periodically be receiving a newsletter that tells about some of the activities your child is doing. You'll also get a few short *Homework Activity* pages, so that your child can "show off" skills learned. We hope this information and the activities will be helpful and informative.

Meet Einstein and Professor Green

A few weeks ago, your child met our frog friends, Einstein and Professor Green. They will help us learn to be better communicators. Einstein helps us learn about the importance of listening at home and at school.

Give Me Five: Stop and Listen

Through the use of the signal *Give Me Five* (hold open a hand), your child can demonstrate a listening position that says to the speaker, "I'm ready to listen and learn!"

Your child should be able to tell or show you how to listen by having eyes on the speaker, mouth quiet, body still, ears listening, and hands free. (We talked about the importance of having our brain working too.)

We practiced being active listeners by signaling when we heard three special words from the story *Let's Go Home, Little Bear*, by Martin Waddell. The students first predicted, or guessed, what they thought might have made the sounds *plop*, *drip*, and *woo*. The students gave a thumbs-up signal whenever one of these words was heard in the story. We discussed the differences between their predictions and the actual source of the sounds as used in the story.

Tune Out Noise!

Your child now knows about ignoring or tuning out distractions when it is important to listen. We practiced this skill when we recorded the story *Too Much Noise*, by Ann McGovern. Each child was assigned a sound effect for a particular animal character in the story. It took a great deal of concentration to *tune out* what the other characters were doing. The students did a *great* job!

Active Listening and Art!

The students practiced being active listeners as we talked about a number of art prints by famous artists, such as Frederic Remington, Winslow Homer, and Horace Pippin. The students had to give a thumbs-up signal whenever I tried to trick them by telling something about the print that did not make sense. The students had to listen and look carefully at the picture and signal whenever they heard a mistake. The students proved to be very careful listeners!

We learned and practiced a very polite way of asking for *clarification* when the information was not clear or might be in error, by saying, "Excuse me, but did you mean to say…" or "Excuse me, but the picture shows a desert not a forest." They were able to demonstrate careful listening in a very polite way!

We Love Clear Directions!

Our final lesson in this unit was to practice giving and following clear, precise directions. We learned to use *specific* words to tell where something was located, such as "Put the big tree in the grass beside the pond" and to ask questions when we did not understand what to do. Targeted vocabulary included *big, little, large, small, in, on, above, below, next to, over, under, right,* and *left,* for example. Color words also helped us be specific when describing.

Ask a Question—Get Information

Homework Activity
We use our question words to gather information
My name: ______
I am interviewing: ______
What is your favorite food? ______
Where were you born? ______
When is your birthday? ______
Who is your hero? ______
Why? ______

The students also practiced identifying and using question words to gain more information. We had fun interviewing, as well as being interviewed by, classmates. It's important to know the difference between *telling* or *commenting* on something and *asking questions* to learn more.

UNIT TWO

IT MAKES SENSE: SIGHT WORDS (PART I)

GOAL

To use precise descriptors in expressive language

BACKGROUND INFORMATION

This lesson begins a series of lessons that work to build "word power" (i.e., vocabulary knowledge and flexibility in word use). The main focus of the *It Makes Sense: Sight Words* lesson is to help students use size, shape, color, and distinctive feature words when describing items that they are observing. Visual information is specifically highlighted in the first two lessons. Other senses are addressed in subsequent *It Makes Sense* lessons. Many academic tasks require students to describe things without the benefit of using all of their senses to gain information, as in an assignment or activity requiring students to describe an object strictly from a picture. In this lesson, students are encouraged to use attributes that are visually observable, although the attribute might also fit another sense (e.g., fuzziness can be both seen and felt).

OBJECTIVES

1. Understand the value of expressing oneself with precise words by developing word power.
2. Use visual descriptors for size, shape, color, and distinctive feature when describing visual characteristics of an object.

MATERIALS

1. Einstein character (Recommended but not necessary; see page 12.)
2. *Five Senses* graphic (See page 88; duplicate and enlarge the graphic, color it, mount it onto colorful construction paper or poster board, and laminate it for durability, if desired.)
3. A bag of assorted candies in wrappers, to be described
4. Social application story: *Einstein Learns about Word Power* (See pages 89–94; also see page 7.)
5. *Sight Words* graphics (See pages 95–96; duplicate and enlarge the graphics, color them, mount them onto colorful construction paper or poster board, and laminate them for durability, if desired.)
6. A basketball, a golf ball, and a marble

INTRODUCTION

Tie-in to Prior Learning

Have Einstein remind the students that they have been working on using their words to give clear directions. He can comment on how beautifully they decorated his pond by putting things in just the right place—above the tree, next to the flower, on the lily pad. Explain that they are CAREful listeners and that they will have to continue to practice these skills as they move on to the next skill.

Focus/Relevancy

Have Einstein ask the students what they can do to become stronger or more powerful people. Let the students share ideas for healthy living, such as good nutrition and exercise. Have Einstein tell them that in this lesson, they are going to discover a way to become stronger, more powerful thinkers and to develop their word power!

LESSON ACTIVITIES

1. Say to the students:

   Today we are going to use our "powers of observation" to make a request. What does observation *mean? I'm going to put an object behind my back. Can you observe what it is?*

   Without modeling a response, have students try to tell what the object is. Ask after each attempt if the student knows for sure or if he or she is just guessing. After several children have made a guess, choose a child to come up to look in your hands and to reveal to the class what you are holding. Have the student explain how he or she could tell what it was. The student should give some type of response indicating that he or she could *see* what it was, or he or she *looked* at it. Stress that in order to *observe* something, you have to look at it with your eyes. Show the *Five Senses* poster. Explain that when you use your eyes, you are using your sense of *sight*.

   HINT

   If working with students who are visually impaired, you may need to encourage them to use their other senses to gather information about an object (e.g., highlight the texture or feel of the object to determine a distinctive feature).

2. Hold up several of the candies, and explain that the students are going to be able to request one of them. Discuss what the word *request* means, and model an example of asking politely (e.g., "May I please get a drink of water?").

   Tell the students that they will be able to request one of the candies but that they may not ask for it by name (i.e., They cannot say, "May I have the Tootsie Roll?" or "May I have the candy?").

   HINT

   Do not explicitly say to students, for example, "Request which candy you want by telling me the color of it." The purpose of this portion of the lesson is to let the children learn on their own the need for precise words to describe the visual attributes of an object.

The students might request the candy by saying, "I want one" or "Give me that one." Do not reward these requests with a candy. Instead, after such attempts, tell the students to use words that tell exactly what they want. After two or three tries, tell the students that they need to learn how to build their word power along with Einstein. (Reassure the students that they will have another opportunity to try out their word power to request a candy.)

3. Read the *Einstein Learns about Word Power* social application story. Let the students make predictions throughout the story, such as what sounds Einstein might hear on his picnic, what could make a "thud, squish" sound, or what the creature is going to do to Professor Green. Let the students help read the sound effect words. Ask the students what strategies Professor Green taught Einstein to use when he did not know how to describe what he was seeing. After all the words have been reviewed, show the *Sight Words* posters for size, shape, color, and distinctive feature. Have students refer to the posters while they look at the candies and list the characteristics that can be seen.

4. Tell the students:

   Einstein learned to tell some valuable information when describing the creature at their picnic. Let's see if you can use some of those powerful words to request a piece of candy again.

   Hold the bag of candies and let each student model a polite request such as, "May I have the candy with the yellow wrapper?" If students name a characteristic that cannot be seen (e.g., "Could I have the sweet treat?"), affirm what they are describing, but ask for a characteristic that can be seen. If they say, "I want *that* one" and point to the candy, tell them that they have to use their words, not their fingers. Remind the students to use their eyes and their powerful words to find a way to request the one they want. As children start to get the right idea by saying that they want the red one or the one with a clear wrapper with white letters, reinforce their responses by saying, for example, "Yes. Dawn described the color. She gets a piece of candy." Students may eat their treat at teacher discretion.

   HINTS

   - The term *distinctive feature* may require more clarification and examples. (Use the golf clap [see page 12] to clap out the syllables while saying the word *di/stinc/tive* together.) Discuss what makes something different or unusual from the things around it. The educator might use the example of someone coming into a classroom and not knowing anyone's name. The visitor would need to describe the students by hair color, clothing, or something that makes them unique from the other students around them. Call on students by naming a distinctive feature, and discuss how he or she knew to stand up (e.g., "Stand up if you are wearing a red shirt with a green dinosaur on it"). Then name a common feature, such as, "If you are wearing blue jeans, please stand up." Ask the students why so many more children are standing this time. Help them realize that this feature is not distinctive because it does not make one person different from everyone else.

- Also, students need to realize that size is a relative term and depends upon the other items to which the item is compared (e.g., a mouse is big when compared to an ant, small when compared to an elephant, and medium-sized in relation to both). Hold up a golf ball and a basketball. Ask if the golf ball is big or small. Then hold up a golf ball and a marble. Ask if the golf ball is big or small. Explain that something can be big or small, depending upon what it is being compared to.

CLOSURE

Summarize the lesson, repeat its relevance to students, and tie it to future learning. Remind students of Einstein's use of powerful words to describe the scary-looking creature. Have the students use their whisper voice to name the four visual descriptors (i.e., size, shape, color, and distinctive feature) as a group. Show the *Five Senses* poster. Explain that in the next lesson, the students will practice more with their sense of sight. In Part II of this lesson, students will practice using these sight words.

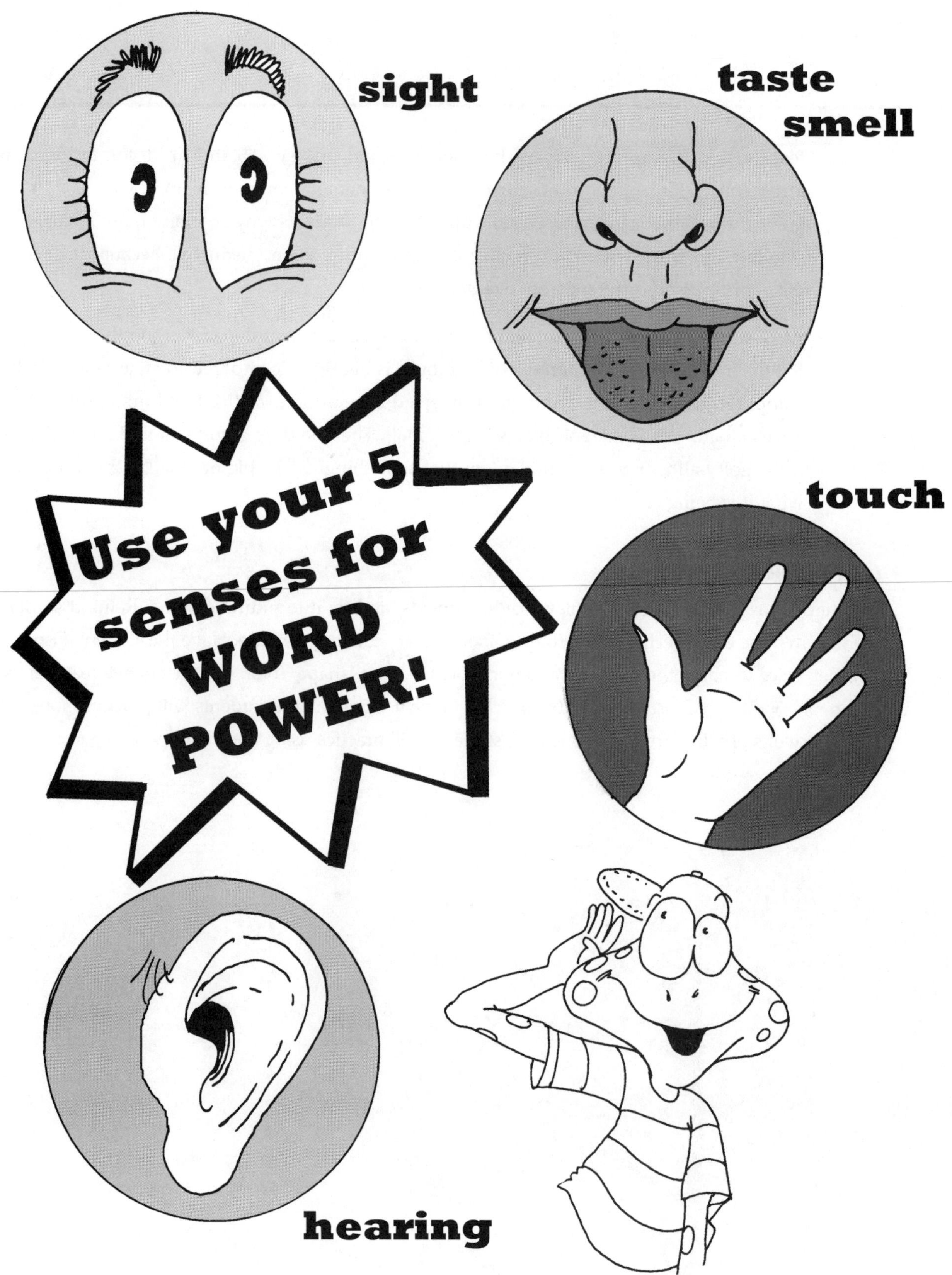
sight
taste
smell
Use your 5 senses for WORD POWER!
touch
hearing

One afternoon, Einstein and Professor Green decided to go for a picnic by the pond.

It was a beautiful day. The sun was shining, and since Einstein was an expert listener, he decided to STOP and LISTEN to the sounds around them.

He heard birds chirping happily in the trees. He heard bees buzzing around the flowers. Then, he heard THUD, SQUISH!

2

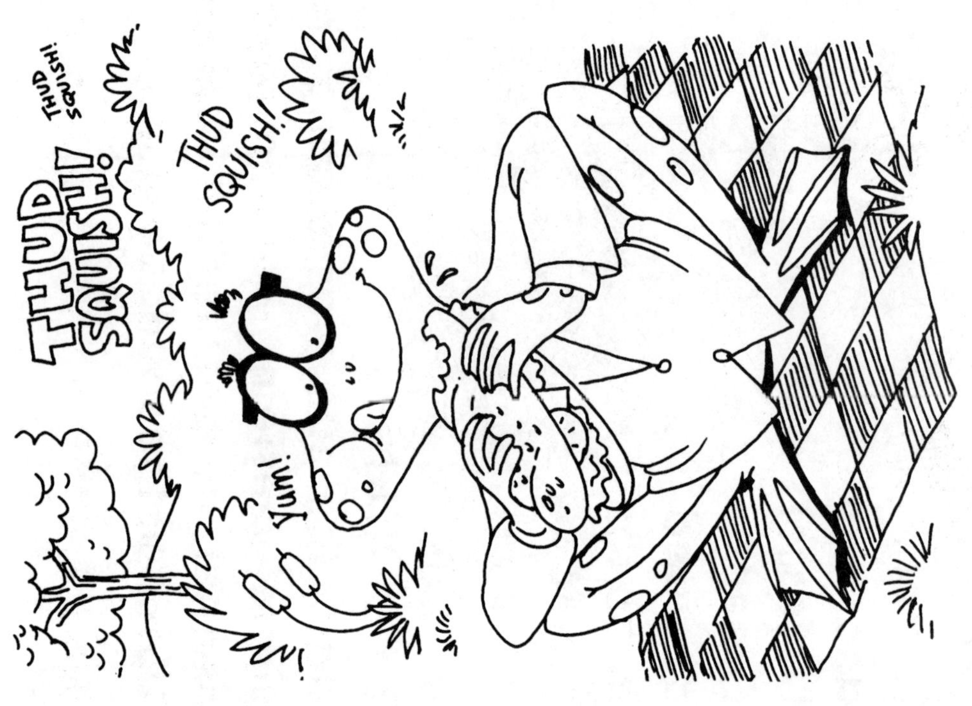

Professor Green was so busy munching on his sandwich that he didn't even hear the sound.

3

When Einstein looked closer, he could see where the sound was coming from. Across the pond, the tall grass shifted with each THUD, SQUISH.

4

Suddenly, Einstein could see a giant creature coming toward them. He tried to tell Professor Green what he was seeing.

"What is it?" Professor Green asked.

5

"It's…
it's…
uh…
well…"

"Einstein, if you don't know what to say, you need WORD POWER. Let's start by telling what size it is."

"Well…it…it's big…it's huge…it's… ENORMOUS!"

Einstein continued, "But…but… um…um…"

6

Professor Green replied, "I see that you have more to tell. Why don't you tell what color it is."

Einstein's eyes were big and he gulped, "It's…gr…gr…green, orange, and purple!"

7

Professor Green could see that Einstein was even more excited than before. He explained, "It also helps to tell the shape of something that you are describing or to tell a distinctive feature. What makes it special?"

8

"It has a large, oval, green body, with purple hair sticking straight up. It has long, sharp teeth, and... it's...it's RIGHT BEHIND YOU!"

9

Professor Green heard lips smacking and snorting sounds behind him. Then he felt a sharp tap on his shoulder.

10

He turned with a start, when the creature suddenly began to speak. "Excuse me," the creature said politely, "do you have the time?"

11

Sight Words

An apple is small.

An apple is round.

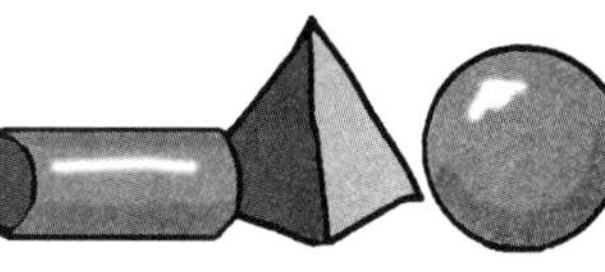

An apple can be red or green.

An apple has a core with seeds.

color

feature

Sight Words

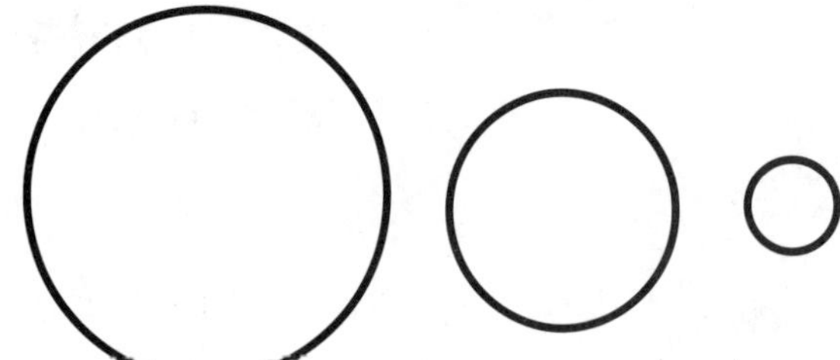

size

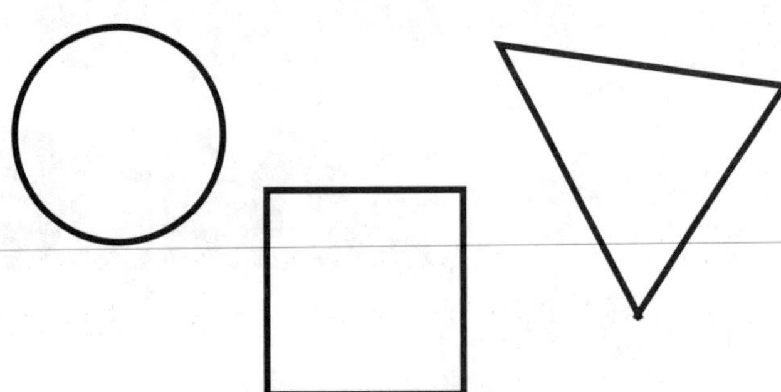

shape

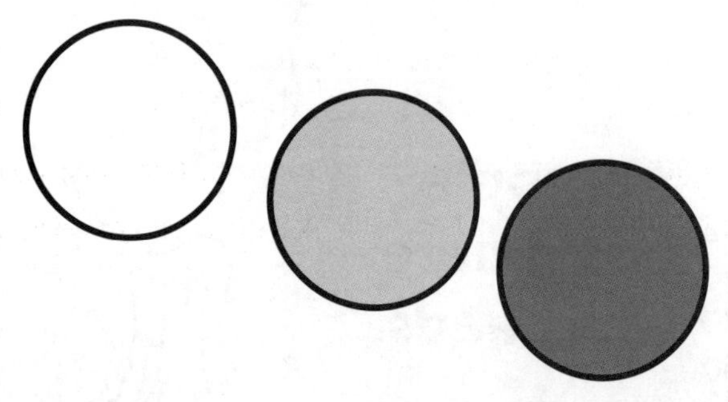

color

distinctive feature

IT MAKES SENSE: SIGHT WORDS (PART II)

GOAL

To use precise descriptors in expressive language

BACKGROUND INFORMATION

The main focus of Part II is to give students an opportunity to practice using size, shape, color, and distinctive feature words when describing visual attributes. Many academic tasks require students to describe things without the benefit of using all of their senses to gain information, as in an assignment or activity requiring students to describe an object strictly from a picture. In this lesson, students are encouraged to use attributes that are visually observable, although the attribute might also fit another sense (e.g., fuzziness can be both seen and felt).

OBJECTIVES

1. Reinforce the value of expressing oneself with precise words by developing word power.
2. Use visual descriptors for size, shape, color, and distinctive feature when describing visual characteristics of an object.

MATERIALS

1. Einstein character (Recommended but not necessary; see page 12.)
2. *Sight Words* posters (Created earlier)
3. Two identical sets of *Occupation Creatures* parts (See pages 99–103; duplicate two sets, color them, cut them apart, and laminate them for durability. Post one set on a chalkboard or magnetic board using tape or magnets.)

INTRODUCTION

Tie-in to Prior Learning

Have Einstein ask what kind of power the students were developing in the last lesson. Elicit the concept of developing word power.

Focus/Relevancy

Have Einstein review the *Sight Words* posters by leading the students in a cheer to emphasize their use of powerful words. Say to the students:

When I tell the size, I'm using…

Students respond...

Word power!

Repeat the cheer for each of the other three visual attributes: shape, color, distinctive feature.

HINT
Einstein or the teacher can encourage the students to respond both verbally and physically, by flexing their powerful arm muscles, as depicted by Einstein on the cover of the social application story *Einstein Learns about Word Power,* while saying the cheer.

LESSON ACTIVITIES

1. Arrange one set of parts for the *Occupation Creatures* in columns on the board, with heads in the first column, bodies in the second, and legs in the third. Place the second set of creature parts at a desk or table in the classroom. Ask the students what they notice about the parts on the board. Lead the students to discover that certain body parts could be put together to create a fire fighter, police officer, etc. As students notice that a variety of occupations are pictured, briefly tell about the five occupations.

   Explain to the students that they will be putting parts together in a different way. They will need to use their word power to describe these new creatures.

2. Select two students at a time. One student goes to the board as "the listener." The other student sits at the desk or table with the second set of creatures and selects a part from either the "head," "body," or "legs" pile to describe for the listener. Guide the students to attend to the attributes that are common to all the parts and those attributes that make the description clear (e.g., if the student only tells that the head is round, point out that several of the heads are round). Although telling the shape is a good describing tool, encourage the student to include the size, color, and distinctive feature.

   Continue in pairs until all the students have had an opportunity to either choose a part or to give a description. As each listener selects the described part, it should be moved to an area where the creature can be built.

CLOSURE

Summarize the lesson, repeat its relevance to students, and tie it to future learning. Praise the students on their ability to use word power just like Einstein learned to used his eyes to help him describe what he was seeing. Tell the students that in the next lesson, they will use their ears to help them describe.

Occupation Creatures

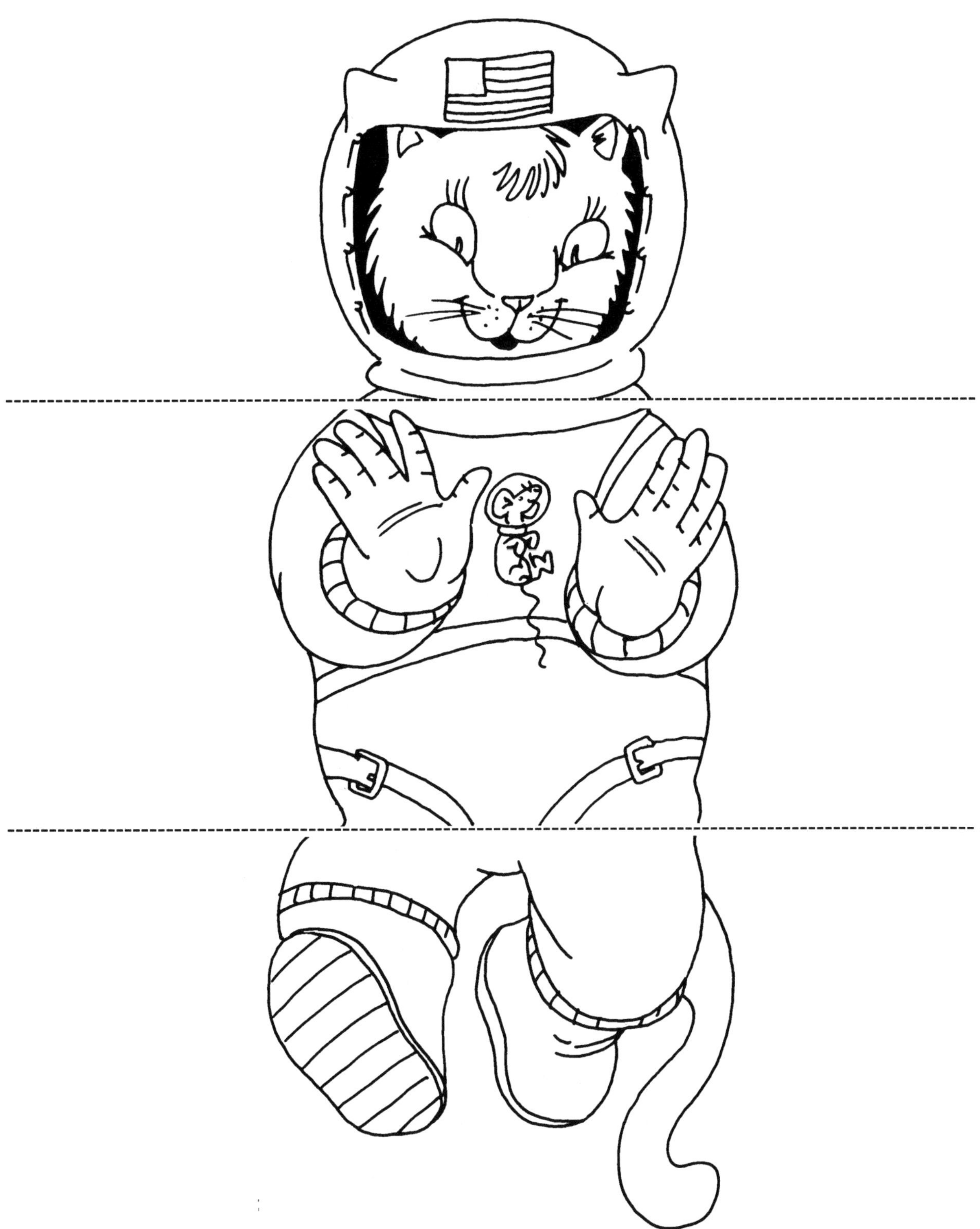

P.D.
P.D.
STOP

IT MAKES SENSE: SOUND WORDS

GOAL

To improve receptive and expressive language skills

BACKGROUND INFORMATION

The *It Makes Sense: Sound Words* lesson is one in a series of lessons that work to build "word power" (i.e., vocabulary knowledge and flexibility in word use). In this lesson, students are encouraged to identify and generate words that describe different sounds (i.e., onomatopoeic words) and to compare and contrast various kinds of sounds.

OBJECTIVES

1. Increase vocabulary by naming words associated with various kinds of sounds.
2. Predict and identify various sound sources and tell whether the sounds are the same or different.

MATERIALS

1. Einstein character (Recommended but not necessary; see page 12.)
2. *The Very Quiet Cricket* (1990), by Eric Carle (Alternatively, use *Listen to the Rain,* 1988, by Bill Martin Jr. and John Archambault, illustrated by James Endicott, or choose any book that lends itself to a discussion about listening. NOTE: This lesson is based on vocabulary from *The Very Quiet Cricket.)*
3. Chalkboard and chalk
4. *Sound Words* graphic (See page 107; duplicate and enlarge the graphic, color it, mount it onto colorful construction paper or poster board, and laminate it for durability, if desired.)
5. Sound shakers (Fill small containers [e.g., film canisters] with various substances such as salt, macaroni, paper clips, beans, coins, or rice. Make some of the shakers identical in order to compare/contrast sounds. Mark these on the lids with colored dots or numbers for easy identification during the lesson.)
6. *Five Senses* poster (Created earlier)

INTRODUCTION

Tie-in to Prior Learning

Have Einstein tell students that in the last lesson, they used their "powers of observation" to describe different heads, bodies, and legs in order to make different kinds of creatures. Ask which sense is used to observe. Elicit *sight*. Let the class recite, using whisper voices, the kinds of powerful words that help us describe with our eyes (i.e., size, shape, color, distinctive feature).

Focus/Relevancy

1. Have Einstein tell the students that in this lesson, they are going to be using another one of their senses that is very important in school. Ask the students what they do when the teacher uses the "give me five" signal. Elicit the concept of listening for important information. Tell the students that in today's lesson, they will learn to use their listening skills to increase their word power by describing what they hear and telling whether sounds are alike or different.

2. Have Einstein ask the students what sound words they might use to describe the sounds around the pond. Give situations to help elicit sound words (e.g., "A fish jumping might make a ___." or "Bugs might make a ___").

The educator may want to compare and contrast sounds that could be loud (e.g., a dog barking) to soft sounds (e.g., a fly buzzing).

LESSON ACTIVITIES

1. Introduce *The Very Quiet Cricket,* by Eric Carle. Highlight the fact that the author is also the illustrator. Ask students to predict what the story will be about based on the cover and/or title of the story. Some students may be familiar with this popular story. Explain that they will be listening to the story in a different way. They will have a listening job. Point out that the author has used many sound words for various creatures who "talk" in the story. (For example, on the first page of the story, the big cricket *chirps* his welcome.) Begin reading the story. After each page, stop to see if they heard the special sound word, and list the identified sound word on the board.

2. Explain that since the students have heard and identified the many sound words that Eric Carle chose for his story, they will now have a chance to think of some sound words on their own. Show the *Sound Words* poster and discuss the familiar sounds pictured and written on the chart. Brainstorm other familiar sounds. You may want to add these to the current list on the board.

3. Say to the students:

> *Now we will really exercise our listening skills by listening to sounds when we don't have pictures to help us decide what they are. Let's be scientists as we use our word power to record the sounds that we hear from these containers and predict what might be inside.*

Pick up a sound shaker container and say to the students:

> *You're a scientist and you've discovered something that sounds like this...* (Shake the canister). *What sound word would describe this sound?*

Record responses on the board. Try to get the students to describe the sound itself before guessing what is making the sound. Elicit a variety of sound words (e.g., *swish, rattle, clank, plink*). After the students have described the type of sound, ask them to predict what is making the sound. Have the students listen to pairs of containers to compare whether they are hearing the same or different sounds, high or low sounds, quiet or loud sounds. Then show them what is inside.

CLOSURE

Summarize the lesson, review its relevance to students, and tie it to future learning. Refer to the impressive list of sound words on the board, and recap how the students used their ears, as well as their eyes, to describe. Explain that they strengthened their word power! Show the *Five Senses* poster. Remind the students that they have practiced describing by observing with their eyes, or seeing (point out the eye on the chart), and observing with their ears, or hearing (point to the ear). Ask the students to predict which of the remaining senses they will learn about next. Keep them in suspense until the next lesson!

Sound Words

ring!
ring!!
crash!
Boom!
rattle
Shake!
Clatter!
drip
drip
drip
plop!

IT MAKES SENSE: TASTE AND SMELL WORDS

GOAL

To improve receptive and expressive language skills

BACKGROUND INFORMATION

The *It Makes Sense: Taste and Smell Words* lesson is one in a series of lessons that work to build "word power" (i.e., vocabulary knowledge and flexibility in word use). In this lesson, students are encouraged to explore several different tastes and smells: sweet, salty, sour. They will identify the three different tastes and generate other items that could fit into each taste/smell group (i.e., categorize).

OBJECTIVES

1. Increase vocabulary by naming words associated with different kinds of tastes and smells.
2. Predict and identify different flavors and odors.

MATERIALS

1. Einstein character (Recommended but not necessary; see page 12.)
2. *Five Senses* poster (Created earlier)
3. *Taste and Smell Words* graphic (See page 112; duplicate and enlarge the graphic, color it, mount it onto colorful construction paper or poster board, and laminate it for durability, if desired.)
4. *Taste and Smell Symbols* (See page 113; duplicate and enlarge the graphic, color it, mount it onto colorful construction paper or poster board, and laminate it for durability, if desired.)
5. *Taste and Smell Recording Charts* (See pages 114–116; duplicate and enlarge the graphics, color them, mount them onto colorful construction paper or poster board, and laminate them for durability, if desired.)
6. Food samples (Use candy, marshmallows, and raisins for sweet samples; pickles, lemons, and limes for sour samples; and pretzels, potato chips, and crackers for salty samples; cut into small pieces, if necessary, and place them in a container until needed.)
7. Two different-colored erasable or water-soluble markers

INTRODUCTION

Tie-in to Prior Learning

Have Einstein remind the students that in the last lesson, they used one of their senses to listen for and give sound words. Continue to use the Einstein character to lead the students in the following discussion: Ask the students to point to the sense organ that is used to listen. Have the students name some of the sound words that they heard in the story *The Very Quiet Cricket* and when listening to the different objects in the sound shakers, such as buzzing, bubbling, swishing, rattling, clunking. Referring to the *Five Senses* poster, talk about the students' developing word power as you review the senses that they have used thus far to describe what they saw and heard. Encourage the students to use specific words when describing something by telling its size, shape, color, and distinctive feature and whether it makes any kind of sound. Ask the students to predict which of the five senses they will practice describing with next.

Focus/Relevancy

Have Einstein tell about his favorite snack by saying:

> *To give you a clue about which two of the five senses we will practice describing with next, I want to describe my favorite snack for you. I love to eat a food that smells* ***sweet****, tastes* ***sugary*** *on the inside,* ***crunchy*** *on the outside, and is covered with* ***salty*** *sprinkles on top. It's a toasted beetle with a crispy mosquito topping!*

Have Einstein ask which two of the five senses he used to describe his snack. Allow several students to respond. To stress that taste and smell are important describing tools, continue to have Einstein lead the discussion. To elicit a discussion of tasting and smelling, and to apply the skill of describing these sensations during an appropriate social situation, have Einstein ask the students if they have ever been to a huge feast (discuss the meaning of the word *feast*). Have the students share ideas about a feast that they attended (e.g., a Thanksgiving dinner, a family reunion picnic, a wedding banquet). Explain that today's lesson will help them develop their word power for describing the wonderful foods that they experience at school, at home, and in restaurants.

LESSON ACTIVITIES

1. Show the students the *Taste and Smell Words* poster. Discuss the three different tastes and smells that they will be identifying. Begin by having the students brainstorm foods (other than the ones shown in the poster) that fit into the groups, *sweet, sour,* or *salty,* and write them on the board.

2. Show the *Taste and Smell Symbols* poster. Help the students make the connection between each symbol and the taste and smell it represents (i.e., sweet might make you smile and say "yum"; sour might make you pucker or grimace; and salty usually makes you thirsty, so you'll want a glass of water). Explain to the students that the senses of taste and smell are connected. If a particular food smells sour, it will probably taste sour too. Ask the students if they have ever noticed that food does not taste the same when they have a cold. The sense of smell plays an important part in how foods taste.

3. Post the three different *Taste and Smell Recording Charts* on the board, and explain that the students will be given things to smell and then taste. Begin with the samples for sweet. Explain that they are to wait until all students have their sample and that they will be using their sense of smell first, followed by taste. Divide the number of students into three rows or groups, and give one group candy, one group marshmallows, and one group raisins. Have the students smell their samples first and then predict the taste. Next, have students taste their samples and decide which of the three tastes corresponds the best. Choose one student from each group to tell how it tasted. Have the rest of the students in the group give the thumbs-up signal if they agree. Complete the charts by drawing a line from each sample item to the designated taste.

   OPTIONAL VARIATION: Have the students role-play scientists who are studying samples. Scientists often have to make predictions about a substance, which, in this case, is a food sample. After the students have smelled the food item, let each group make a prediction about the taste, and mark their prediction on the charts with an erasable or water-soluable marker. After they taste the item, mark the taste with a different-colored marker. Discuss whether their senses of smell and taste were the same.

   HINT

   It is helpful to explain to the students that they don't have to taste an item if it smells disagreeable to them. Collect any uneaten samples.

4. Repeat Activity 3 with the other two tastes. (Using the sequence of sweet, salty, sour has been successful for the authors.)

5. Once all three sets of food samples have been recorded, review the original list for each flavor on the board. Let the students generate words or phrases to describe the smells for each group of foods (e.g., sweet: *smells sugary, like candy, like flowers, like honey;* sour: *smells tart, tangy, bitter;* salty: *smells like the ocean, like a brine, like smoked meat*).

6. Help the students put the lists into sentence form (e.g., "The pickles, lemons, and limes are alike because they are all sour" or "The pretzels, crackers, and potato chips are alike because they are all salty") and say the sentences aloud as a group.

CLOSURE

Summarize the lesson, review its relevance to students, and tie it to future learning. Refer to the impressive list of taste and smell words on the board, and recap how the students used their nose and their taste buds to describe and strengthen their word power! Show the *Five Senses* chart. Remind the students that they have practiced describing by observing with their eyes, or seeing (point out the eye on the graphic), by using their ears, or hearing (point to the ear), and, in today's lesson, by using their tongue and nose for tasting and smelling (point to the tongue and nose on the poster) to describe different foods. Ask the students which of the five senses is left. Elicit *touch,* which students will use in the next lesson to strengthen their word power.

Taste and Smell Words

sweet

sour

salty

Taste and Smell Symbols

sweet

---

sour

---

salty

Taste and Smell Recording Charts

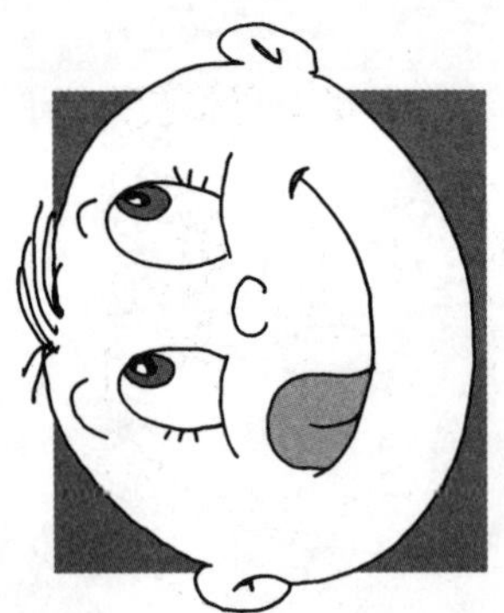

sweet

sour

salty

cracker

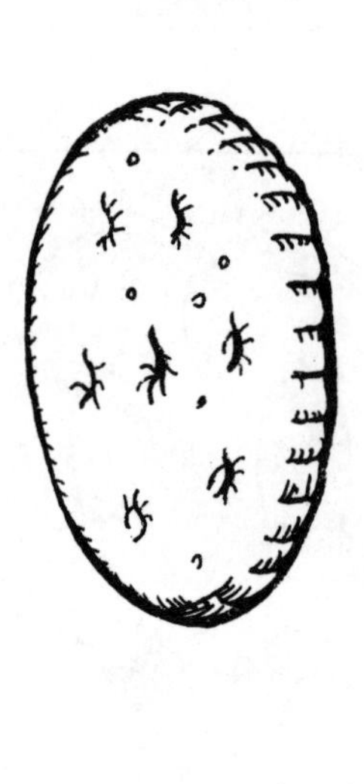

marshmallow

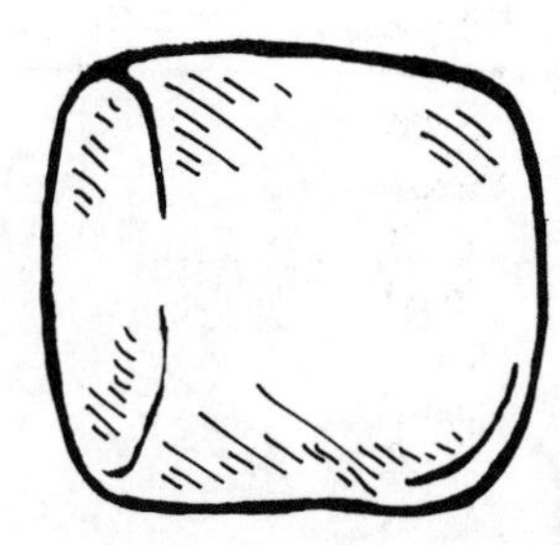

pickle

candy

potato chip

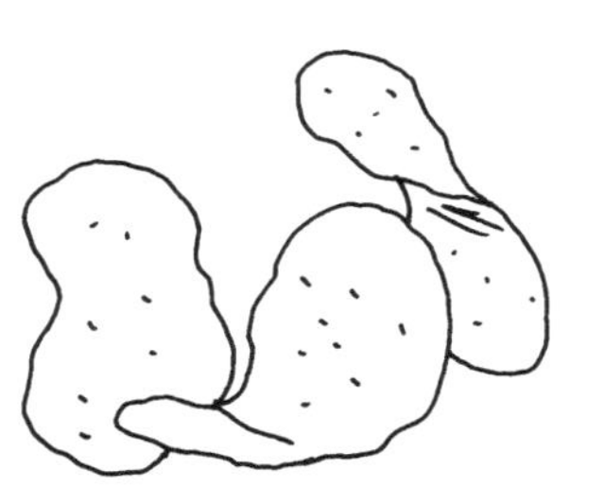

lemon

sweet

sour

salty

sweet

sour

salty

pretzel

lime

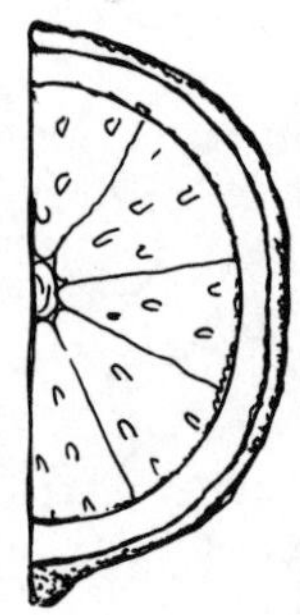

raisin

IT MAKES SENSE: TOUCH WORDS

GOAL

To improve receptive and expressive language skills

BACKGROUND INFORMATION

The *It Makes Sense: Touch Words* lesson is one in a series of lessons that work to build "word power" (i.e., vocabulary knowledge and flexibility in word use). In this lesson, students are encouraged to explore the sense of touch by generating words to describe various objects. This lesson also emphasizes the four seasons as a tie-in to the kindergarten and first grade curricula.

OBJECTIVES

1. Increase vocabulary by naming words associated with the sense of touch.
2. Identify and describe different textures.

MATERIALS

1. Einstein character (Recommended but not necessary; see page 12.)
2. Seasonal/predictable poems (See pages 120–123; duplicate and enlarge the poems, color them, mount them onto colorful construction paper or poster board, and laminate them for durability, if desired.)
3. Objects to touch associated with the four seasons: ice cubes within a closed baggie, pine cones, seashells, and cotton balls that have been rolled and stretched to represent caterpillars. (If used in a classroom, have at least three or four of each item to be passed around.)
4. An erasable or water-soluble marker
5. *Touch Words* graphic (See page 124; duplicate and enlarge the graphic, color it, mount it onto colorful construction paper or poster board, and laminate it for durability, if desired.)
6. *Five Senses* poster (Created earlier)

INTRODUCTION

Tie-in to Prior Learning

Have Einstein remind students that in the last lesson, they used their senses of smell and taste to describe different food samples (or "scientific samples" if you had the students pretend they were scientists) by determining whether the samples were sweet, sour, or salty. Ask which sense organs are used for smelling and tasting. Remind the students of some of the powerful words they discovered that described their smelling and tasting experience (e.g., *sweet, sour, salty, bitter, tart*). Einstein can tell the students that in this lesson, they are going to be using another one of their senses that is very important in school: their sense of touch.

Focus/Relevancy

1. Have Einstein tell the students that when he stuck his toe in the pond for his morning swim, he discovered that he needed to put on his special insulated swimsuit and fins to keep warm. Have him ask the students how the water must have felt. Einstein can explain that we can touch and feel with more than our fingers because our skin also sends a message to the brain that helps us know whether it is warm enough for a swim or cold enough for frost.
2. Have Einstein tell the students that they can be scientists every day, even when they're not in a laboratory, by observing what's around them with all their senses. Discuss different places where the students could use their senses to learn more about their surroundings (e.g., while working at school, while playing in the park, or whenever they discover something new or different to explore).

LESSON ACTIVITIES

1. Explain to the students that they will be using some special poems to help them discover words to describe how things feel. Introduce the first poem. (Choose the poem that coincides with the current season.) Read the poem several times until the entire class can recite it together using the visual clues. Then pass the corresponding touch object to the students.

   HINT
   Placing the students in rows or small circle groups for this lesson makes passing the items easier to control. It is helpful to have the same number of objects as rows or groups of students.

   Have the students generate words as they feel each object, and list them with an erasable or water-soluble marker directly on the laminated poem. Reread the poem including the feeling words that the students have generated.

2. Choose a second poem to read. Repeat Activity 1. After the second poem has been read, ask the students if they have noticed a pattern. If no one responds, continue on with the next two poems, but tell the students to listen and watch for a pattern. Repeat Activity 1 for the third and fourth poems. After all the poems have been read, discuss the sentence pattern within the poems (e.g., "It was a [*chilly*/*snowy*/*rainy*/*sunny*] day when we went out to play"), as well as the seasonal patterns illustrated by the four poems (i.e., *chilly*—fall, *snowy*—winter, etc.). Have the students name the seasons.

3. Review the different "feeling" words that have been written on each poem. Show the *Touch Words* poster and read the words together with the students. Compare to see if all the words on the poems are also on the *Touch Words* poster. If the poster has any different words, add them to the poems. Reread each poem with the complete list of "feeling" words.

CLOSURE

Summarize the lesson, review its relevance to students, and tie it to future learning. Refer to the impressive list of "feeling" words written on each poem, and recap how the students used their sense of touch to describe and strengthen their word power. Show the *Five Senses* poster. Einstein can remind the students that they have practiced describing by observing with their eyes, or seeing (point to the eye on the chart), with their ears, or hearing (point to the ear), with their noses, or smelling (point to the nose), with their tongues, or tasting (point to the tongue), and now with their hands, or touching (point to the hand). Tell the students that in the next lesson, they will be using all of their scientific skills and word power to discover the secrets inside some special packages by using all five of their senses!

AChilly Day

It was a chilly day

When we went out to play.

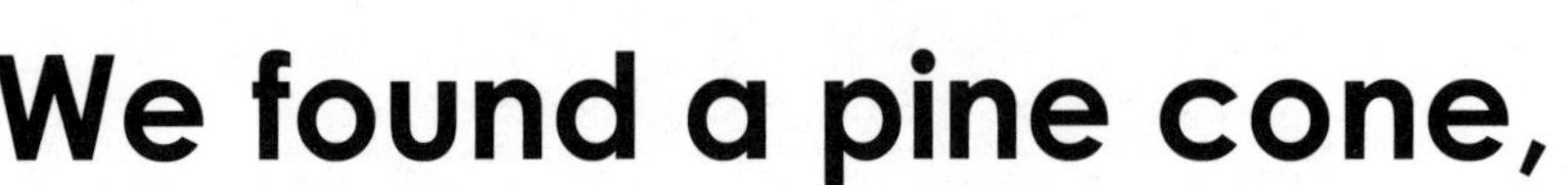

The leaves were falling down.

We found a pine cone,

And it felt...

A Snowy Day

It was a snowy day

When we went out to play.

The flakes were falling down.

We found an icicle,

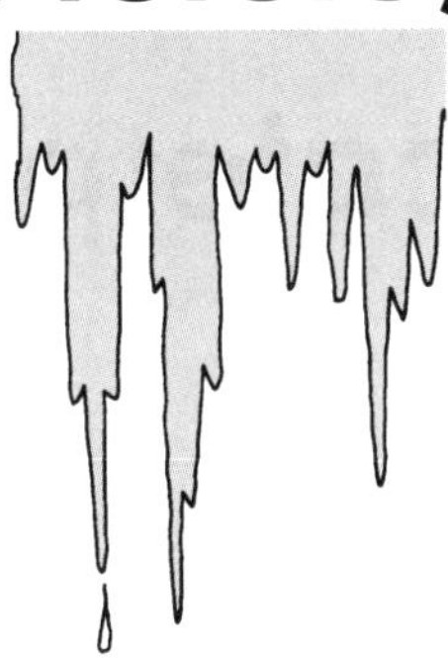

And it felt...

A Rainy Day

It was a rainy day

When we went out to play.

The flowers were
beginning to bloom.

We found a caterpillar,

And it felt...

A Sunny Day

It was a sunny day

When we went out to play.

The sand was burning hot.

We found a seashell,

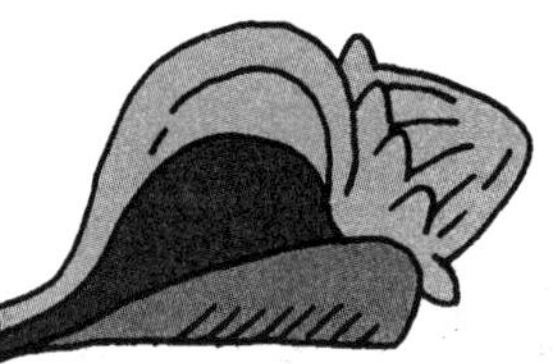

And it felt…

Touch Words

pine cone

hard
sharp
prickly

seashell

hard
rough
pointy

soft
fuzzy
hairy
squishy
tickly

cold
hard
wet
slippery

icicle

caterpillar

IT MAKES SENSE: SUMMARY

GOAL

To improve receptive and expressive language skills

BACKGROUND INFORMATION

The *It Makes Sense: Summary* lesson allows students to practice using vocabulary related to all five senses, along with reviewing the use of question words to gather information.

OBJECTIVES

1. Review the five senses by using related vocabulary when describing various items.
2. Practice asking questions to gather information.

MATERIALS

1. Einstein character (Recommended but not necessary; see page 12.)
2. Sense posters (*Sight Words, Sound Words, Taste and Smell Words, Touch Words*) (Created earlier)
3. Paper bags, each containing a different object related to the first Thanksgiving feast in North America (e.g., Indian corn, an apple, seeds, plastic or glass beads)
4. Chalkboard and chalk

INTRODUCTION

Tie-in to Prior Learning

Have Einstein remind the students of the lesson in which they had to request a special piece of candy using only their "powers of observation." Review the kinds of information that the students used to identify their candy choice visually (i.e., size, shape, color, and distinctive feature). Remind the students that they now have even more word power because they can also tell how it sounds, tastes, smells, or feels. Have Einstein ask the students how they could request, or politely ask, for an object if they could not see it. Tell them that will be their job in today's lesson. Once more, they can be scientists.

Focus/Relevancy

Have Einstein tell about a special package that Professor Green brought to Frog School. The professor would not tell any of the frogs what was inside but told them that if they used their word power, he was sure they could figure out the secret. Ask if any of the students know how to solve Einstein's problem. Point to the sense posters and read the words on the posters as a clue for gathering different kinds of information. Remind the students that in the lesson on gathering information, in which they wondered about something, there was something they could do. Ask what Einstein did when he wondered about the "secret visitor" who was coming to the pond. Elicit the concepts that Einstein should request information or use his question words to gather information and that he should use his five senses to figure out what is in the box. Explain to the students that they will be using their question words and their "powerful" sense words to discover some secrets in today's lesson. Call on several students to tell the question words, and write them on the board.

LESSON ACTIVITIES

1. Have Einstein talk about the difficulties the Pilgrims faced in the 1600s when they went to North America. Remind the students that this was before there were stores and cars and electricity. They needed some kind of shelter, or home, to protect them from the cold weather. They needed food since there was no Tom Thumb or Albertson's (use the names of any familiar grocery stores). The Pilgrims needed warm clothing and other necessities for survival. The Native Americans helped the Pilgrims learn ways to survive there. Say or have Einstein say:

   We are going to pretend that you are a group of Pilgrims who have come to live in America. I am going to pretend to be a Native American with some items that should be helpful to you. I cannot tell you the names of the items, but you can ask questions to help figure them out. For example, you could ask about how the item looks—its color, shape, size, and distinctive feature; how it feels; whether it is something to eat, and how it tastes; how it smells; and whether it makes a sound. If you ask the right kind of questions, I bet you can solve the mystery.

2. Place the first bag with an object inside in front of the students. Tell them to ask questions that will help them figure out what is in the bag. Record on the board the information that is generated from the questions asked by the class. Review periodically what the students have discovered through their questioning (e.g., the mystery items are small, red, and blue; oval in shape, with a hole in the middle; hard; not to be eaten, and have no smell; make a "clinking" sound when the bag is shaken).

   HINT
   You may have to keep the students from trying to guess too quickly by saying:

   *Do you **know** that the secret is beads, or are you **guessing**? Let's gather some more information before we make a guess. What other questions could we ask to find out more?*

   Continue the activity until all the items have been identified.

CLOSURE

Summarize the lesson, repeat its relevancy to students, and tie it to future learning. Have Einstein say to the students:

> *We have been exploring our world by using some very important tools that help us learn and discover new information, just like scientists. These tools will help us as we continue to learn at school and also at home. In a whisper voice, let's name our five senses together.* (Allow time for the students to respond.) *In our next lesson, we are going to have another opportunity to review and practice using our five senses to make discoveries about our world.*

STRATEGY REVIEW LESSON 2

GOAL

To reinforce and review the strategies for "word power" (i.e., vocabulary knowledge and flexibility in word use)

BACKGROUND INFORMATION

The main focus of this lesson is to review the word power strategies: *It Makes Sense: Sight Words, It Makes Sense: Sound Words, It Makes Sense: Taste and Smell Words, It Makes Sense: Touch Words*. A review lesson is provided after several strategies have been taught. In addition, the students take home the *Homework Activity* page and *Communication Skills Newsletter No. 2* to encourage family involvement and understanding of the language skills.

OBJECTIVES

1. Review and practice the major components of the *It Makes Sense: Sight Words, It Makes Sense: Sound Words, It Makes Sense: Taste and Smell Words,* and *It Makes Sense: Touch Words* strategies.
2. Complete the application activities.
3. Share strategy information with family members.

MATERIALS

1. Einstein character (Recommended but not necessary; see page 12.)
2. Sense posters *(Sight Words, Sound Words, Taste and Smell Words, Touch Words)* (Created earlier)
3. *Homework Activity* page (See page 130; duplicate for each student.)
4. *Skills Checklist* (See page 131; duplicate and enlarge the checklist, color it, mount it onto colorful construction paper or poster board, and laminate it for durability, if desired.)
5. *Communication Skills Newsletter No. 2* (See pages 132–133; duplicate for each student.)

INTRODUCTION

Tie-in to Prior Learning

Einstein can remind the students that they have been learning many important skills to help them develop word power. Display and briefly review the sense posters and strategies for these lessons.

Focus/Relevancy

Einstein can remind the students about the last time they had homework and compliment the students on what a good job they did teaching their families about listening. He can tell them that they are going to have another special homework assignment, to be worked on with an older family member. Tell the students that their families will be really impressed with all the information they can share about using their senses!

LESSON ACTIVITIES

1. Show the students the *Homework Activity* page. Relate the questions on the page to the sense posters.
2. Have Einstein select several students to model answers for the class, or have the entire class give choral responses to his review questions from the *Homework Activity* page.
3. Display the *Skills Checklist.* Review the key components of a lesson while looking at the poster and by practicing some items from the *Homework Activity* page. Place or have students place a checkmark on the line beside each skill as the review is completed.
4. Show the students *Communication Skills Newsletter No. 2.* Explain that even their parents have homework. The newsletter describes the activities that they have been doing in class.
5. Hand out the *Homework Activity* page and *Communication Skills Newsletter No. 2* for the students to take home, or place them in envelopes for students to take home.

CLOSURE

Summarize the lesson, repeat its relevance to students, and tie it to future learning. Have Einstein encourage the students to share their *Home Activity* page and *Communication Skills Newsletter No. 2* with someone special at home. Explain that after they have completed the homework, they should have their parent or caregiver sign and date in the appropriate space and return it for a reward (e.g., a sticker or points on a homework chart). Just like Einstein discovered the need to use his senses to describe the strange creature that appeared at his picnic with Professor Green, the students used their word power to describe by using their five senses. Have all the students name the five senses together using a whisper voice. Tell the students that in the next lesson, they will be learning about using symbols to communicate their ideas.

Homework Activity

Name: ______________________________

1. Use the chart below to help you name your five senses!

____

____

2. Describe an egg by telling size, shape, color, and distinctive feature!

size, shape, color, distinctive feature

____

____

____

____

____

____

____

3. You smell cookies baking. How do you think they will taste?

sweet, sour, salty

____

____

____

____

____

____

4. Use your sense of touch to describe your favorite pet!

pine cone, seashell, icicle, caterpillar

____

____

____

____

____

5. What sound words go with each of the following: cat, coffee pot, doorbell?

ring! ring!, crash!, Boom!, rattle, Shake!, clatter!, drip drip drip, plop!

____

____

____

____

____

____

WORD POWER CHALLENGE! Use ALL of your senses to describe popcorn!

____

____

____

____

____

____

Family Member: ______________________ Date: ______________

Skills Checklist

☐ I know my five senses.

☐ I can tell how something looks.

☐ I can give “taste” words.

☐ I can give “touch” words.

☐ I can give “sound” words.

Now I’m ready to learn more about words!

Communication Skills Newsletter

No. 2

Fun with Words!

We have had fun, along with our friends Einstein and Professor Green, discovering how using our senses can help us describe different objects or events with clear, precise words. We used our observational skills when requesting a piece of candy for a treat. We could not ask for the candy by name, so we learned how to ask for the *small* one; the *round* one; the *red, green,* or *purple* one; or the one with a *clear wrapper and white letters.*

Ask your child to tell you which sense we use when we look at something (*seeing* or *sight*). I bet your child can also tell you a *distinctive feature* (what makes an object or person different from the things or people around it). We have stressed the fact that when people use clear, precise describing words, our listeners can picture what we're talking about.

The Sense of Hearing

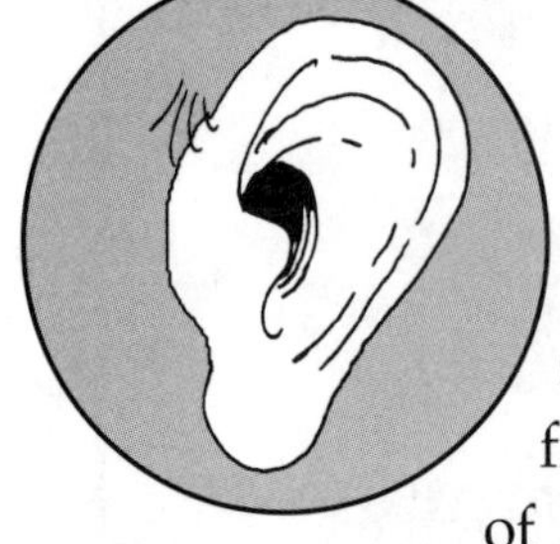

Your child has been learning about the sense of hearing. We first named the kinds of sounds heard during a thunderstorm and then listened to the story *The Very Quiet Cricket,* by Eric Carle. The author used different sound words for the characters in the story. The cicadas *screeched* and the mosquitoes *buzzed*. We talked about describing sounds (e.g., *boom, crash, rattle, swish, clank*) during our listening job, which was to identify the kind of sounds we heard when containers with unknown objects inside of them were shaken (e.g., Was it loud or soft? Did it *rattle* like beans or *swish* like rice?). It was fun to guess what was inside, and then to see if we were correct. We also had to compare whether any of the sounds were the same or different.

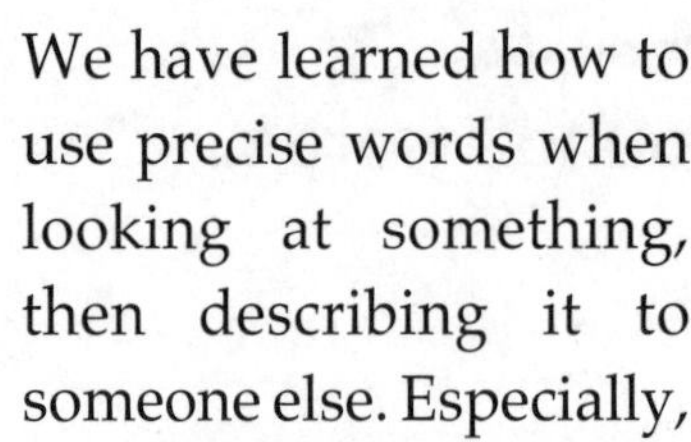

The Sense of Sight

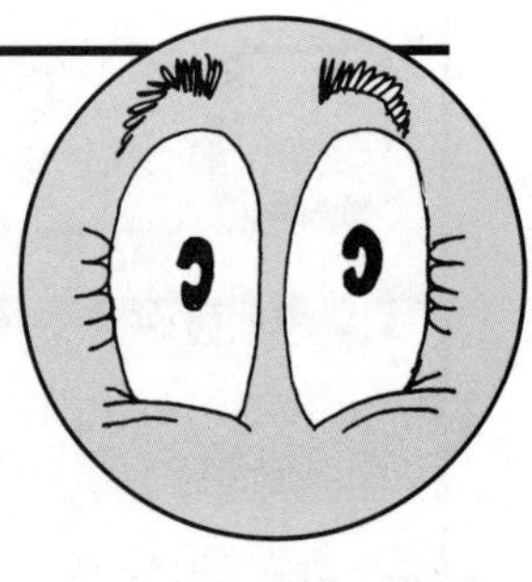

We have learned how to use precise words when looking at something, then describing it to someone else. Especially, we have learned words that tell an object's size, shape, color, and distinctive feature. The distinctive feature is what sets the object apart from everything else. Look around your child's bedroom. Talk about what makes it different from other rooms.

Taste and Smell Senses

Each of us worked in a group to chart the taste and smell findings for our food samples. (Just like scientists!) Each group had to smell and then taste a variety of foods to determine whether they were *sweet, sour,* or *salty*. We then had to chart the type of taste, and smell, for each of the food samples.

We talked about the relationship between the sense of *smell* and the sense of *taste*. (Food just doesn't taste the same when you have a terrible cold!) Because many children seem to be confused, especially between *sweet* and *salty*, talk about the different tastes and smells of foods at home. (For example, "These chips are really salty. Can you think of some other foods that taste salty?" or "Find three foods that smell sweet. Do they taste sweet too?")

Using ALL of Our Senses

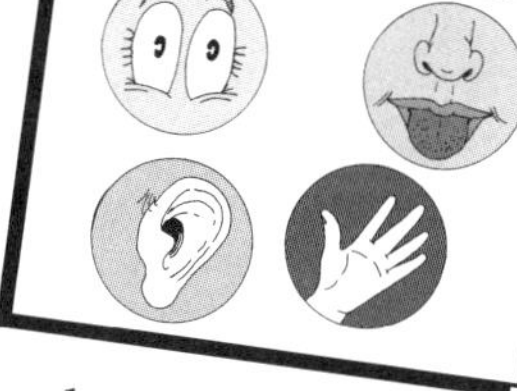

The students practiced using all of their senses to gather information and play a guessing game. We pretended to be Pilgrims in the 1600s. I pretended to be a Native American with some items that the Pilgrims (students) really needed. They guessed what I had in different bags by gathering information through asking questions about its color, shape, size, distinctive feature, sound, taste, smell, or texture. They asked great questions! Ask your child what we found in the bags.

The Sense of Touch

We studied the sense of touch by reading four short poems that followed a predictable pattern. Each poem told about a different season of the year and named something you might find to touch when outside playing. We felt and described a pine cone, ice cube "icicles," a cotton ball "caterpillar," and a seashell. We discovered wonderful describing words, like *prickly, sharp, rough, pointy, wet, slippery, fuzzy, squishy,* and *hairy*.

A Chilly Day

It was a chilly day
When we went out to play.
The leaves were falling down.
We found a pine cone,
And it felt...

A Sunny Day

It was a sunny day
When we went out to play.
The sand was burning hot.
We found a seashell,
And it felt...

Talk at Home

I hope these activities will give you some ideas to try at home. Be sure that your child uses specific language to express wants and needs. If your child doesn't know the word for something, see if he or she can describe the item, and then you may be able to help by supplying the needed word.

SYMBOLS HAVE MEANING

GOAL

To improve receptive and expressive language skills

BACKGROUND INFORMATION

The *Symbols Have Meaning* lesson begins a series of lessons that help students develop vocabulary and higher level thinking skills, including interpreting symbols, categorizing, using synonyms, and comparing and contrasting. These lessons also work to build "word power" (i.e., vocabulary knowledge and flexibility in word use).

An important skill for early classroom success is being aware of the language associated with learning to read or interpret symbolic information. This lesson specifically targets the concept that symbols can be used to represent ideas (e.g., a flag can represent a country, a cake with candles can represent a birthday, a number can represent how many of something, or a letter can represent a sound). The idea of using some type of symbol that will last over time to share one's ideas is also addressed.

OBJECTIVES

1. Build an understanding of symbolic representation through pictures, letters, words, and numbers.
2. Participate in a choral reading activity by interpreting the symbols.

MATERIALS

1. Einstein character (Recommended but not necessary; see page 12.)
2. *Five Senses* poster (Created earlier)
3. *Symbols Have Meaning* graphic (See page 137; duplicate and enlarge the graphic, color it, mount it onto colorful construction paper or poster board, and laminate it for durability, if desired.)
4. Chalkboard and chalk
5. *Picture Symbols* (See pages 138–140; duplicate and enlarge the graphics, color them, mount them onto colorful construction paper or poster board, and laminate them for durability, if desired.)
6. *A Story of Friendship* (See pages 141–144; duplicate and enlarge each page, color the symbols, and make them into a "Big Book" by creating holes with a paper punch and then binding together the pages with string or yarn.)

INTRODUCTION

Tie-in to Prior Learning

Have Einstein remind the students about how they have gained word power by using their five senses to describe what they see or do. Review the *Five Senses* poster. Have Einstein model or lead the students in a description of a roasted turkey (hot, brown, large, juicy, etc.) and an apple or pumpkin pie (sweet, golden, smells like cinnamon, etc.).

Focus/Relevancy

Have Einstein tell about how he and his frog family recently had a special visit from his grandparents to celebrate a special pond holiday. Ask the students what holiday they think about when they see this symbol: (draw a turkey on the board, or show a picture of a turkey). Let a few students share something about their Thanksgiving holiday.

OPTIONAL VARIATION: For those students who do not celebrate Thanksgiving, draw a symbol for a holiday in their culture. Have students share what they do on that holiday.

Highlight the word *symbol* and discuss how some objects or pictures are so strongly associated with places or events that we automatically think of them when we see that particular symbol. Other examples might be the golden arches for McDonalds, a cake with candles for birthdays, an American flag for the USA, and traffic lights for stop, slow down, and go. Have students look around the room and point out examples of symbols.

LESSON ACTIVITIES

1. Explain that there are many symbols used at school. Draw three circles on the board. Explain that your circles are picture symbols that stand for apples. Ask the students to show with their fingers a symbol for how many apples were drawn. They should hold up three fingers. Explain that numbers are symbols for telling "how many." Ask for a volunteer to go up to the board and write the symbol that would represent how many circles are there. The student should write the digit *3* on the board. Then write the word *three* on the board, and explain that words are symbols representing other objects, people, actions, etc. Show the *Symbols Have Meaning* poster and place it where everyone can see it. Review with the class the different types of symbols that are displayed on the poster.

2. Explain that before people communicated with written words, they communicated through picture symbols. Show the *Picture Symbols* posters. Ask the students who might have made up the symbols pictured. (Prompt for people who lived a long time ago or people who don't have a way to write down words.) Explain that one group who used picture symbols in the past is Native Americans, and that they had very good ways to picture important events they wanted to tell about. Ask what kind of picture symbols they might draw to tell about a great hunt (elicit animals, deer tracks, people, arrows, spears). Have the students predict what the symbols on the

Picture Symbols posters might mean. Discuss each symbol and explain that students will be using the symbols to read a story. It is a true story about a group of people called Pilgrims, who travelled across the ocean to live in a new land. They learned to survive thanks to the help of the Native Americans.

3. Present *A Story of Friendship*. Have the students apply their new knowledge while "reading" the picture symbols in the story. All the students should chorally read the pictures; however, some students may also be able to read the other words along with you. Reread the story several more times.

CLOSURE

Summarize the lesson, repeat its relevance to students, and tie it to future learning. Praise the students for their use of symbols to read a story. Challenge them to tell about an important event in their life by using picture symbols, words, or both! Examples might be a special holiday, event, birthday, or even telling how a broken arm came about. If time allows, assist students with this task. Tell the students that in the next lesson, they will gain more word power by lassoing the word herd.

Symbols Have Meaning

Picture Symbols

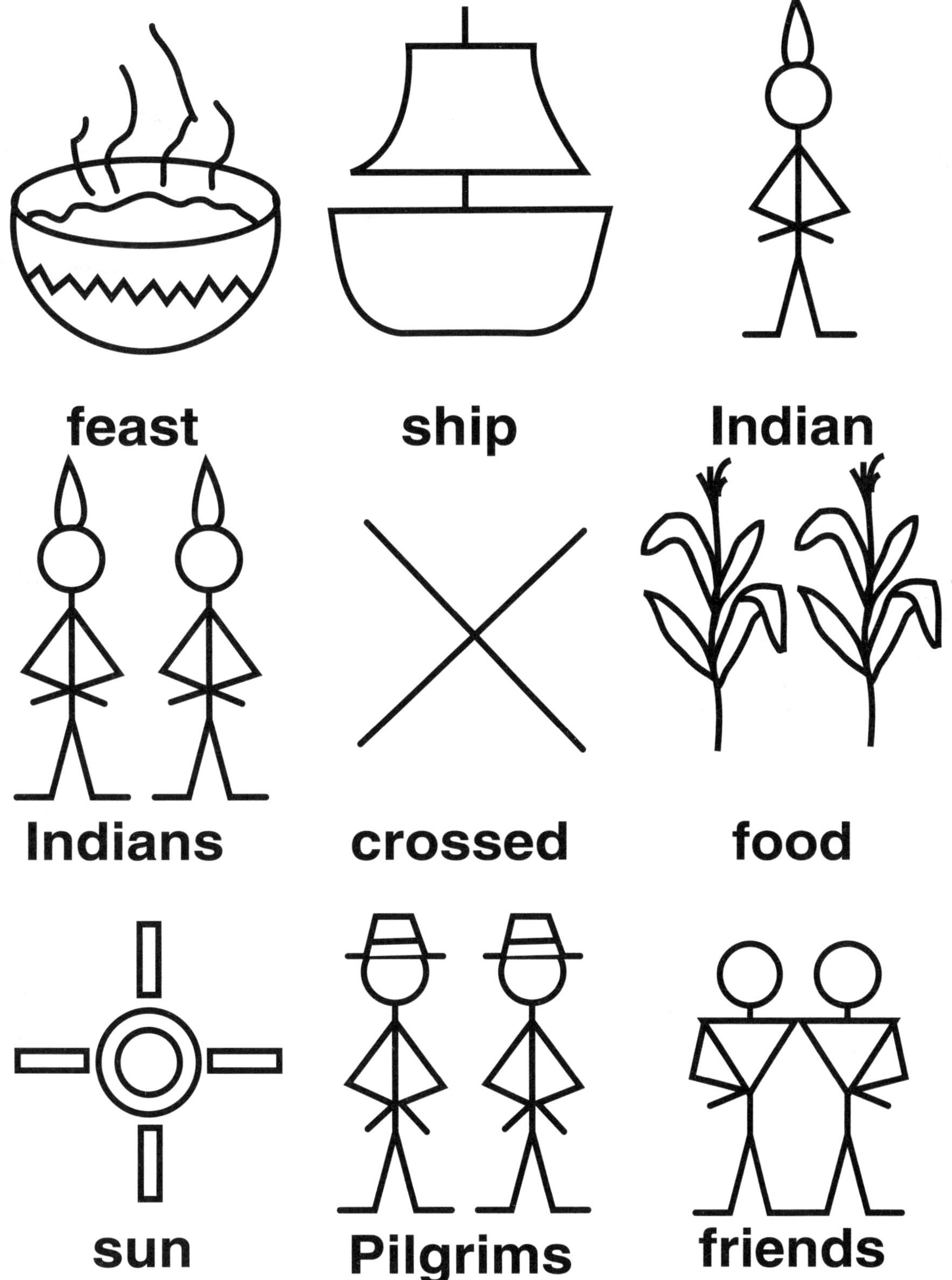
feast
ship
Indian
Indians
crossed
food
sun
Pilgrims
friends

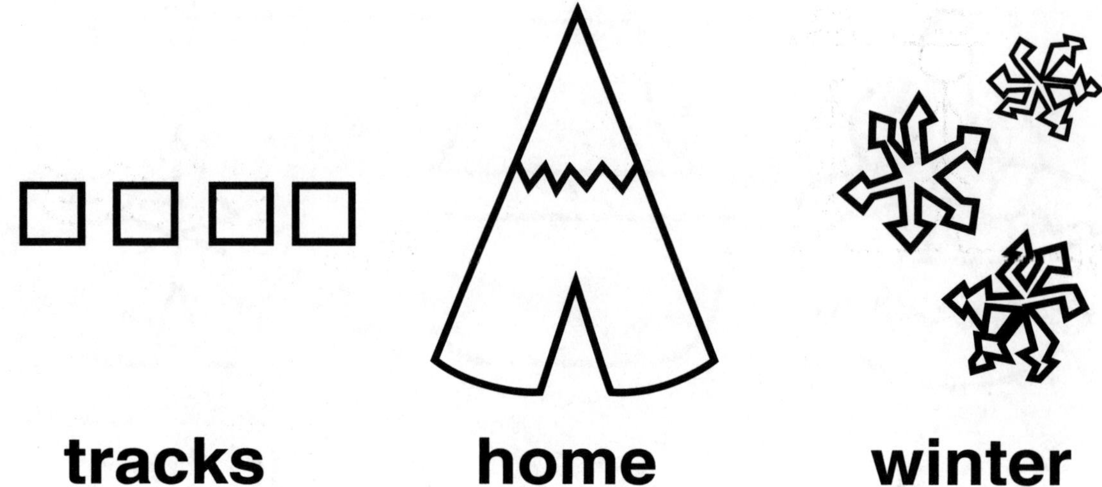
tracks
home
winter

A Story of Friendship

The   the

for many in a .

Making a new was very hard

because the did not have

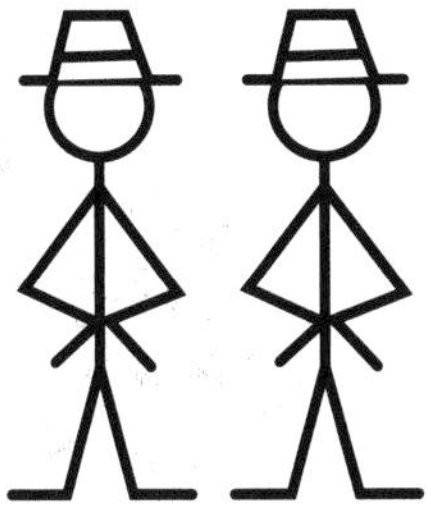

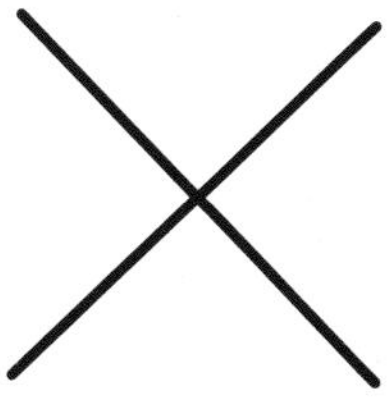

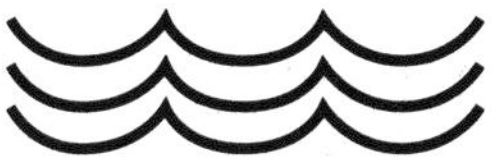

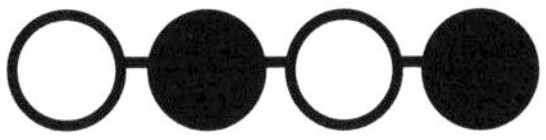

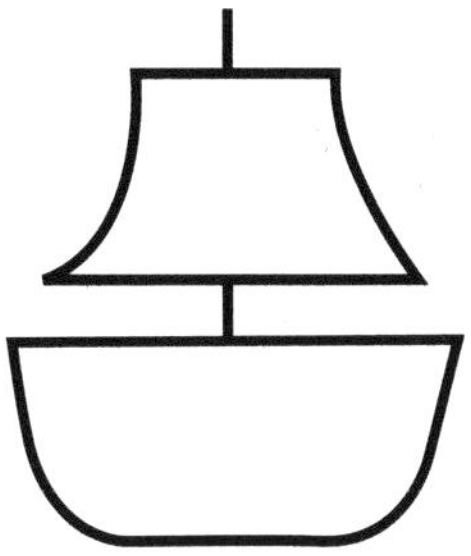

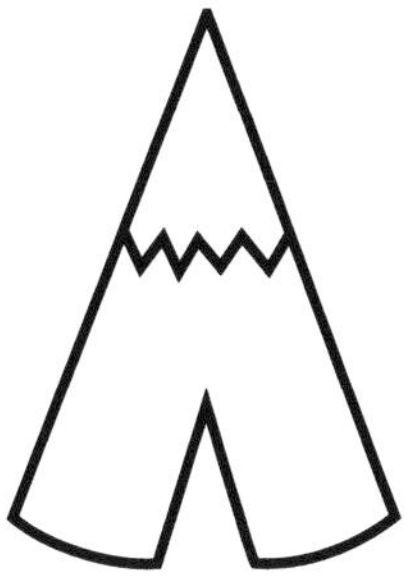

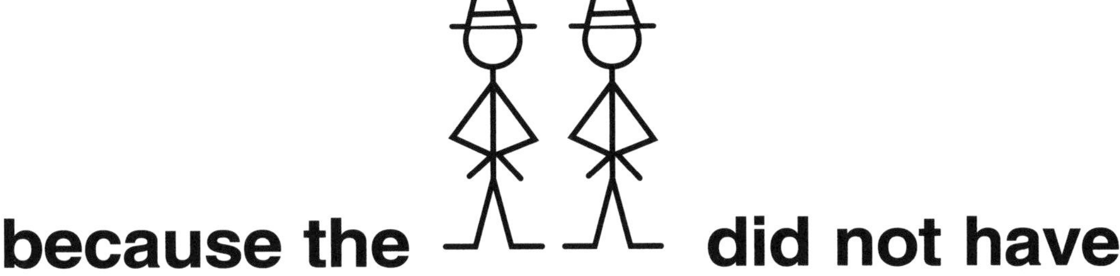

enough  to last through the

 . The  and 

became  . The  knew

which  and  had the

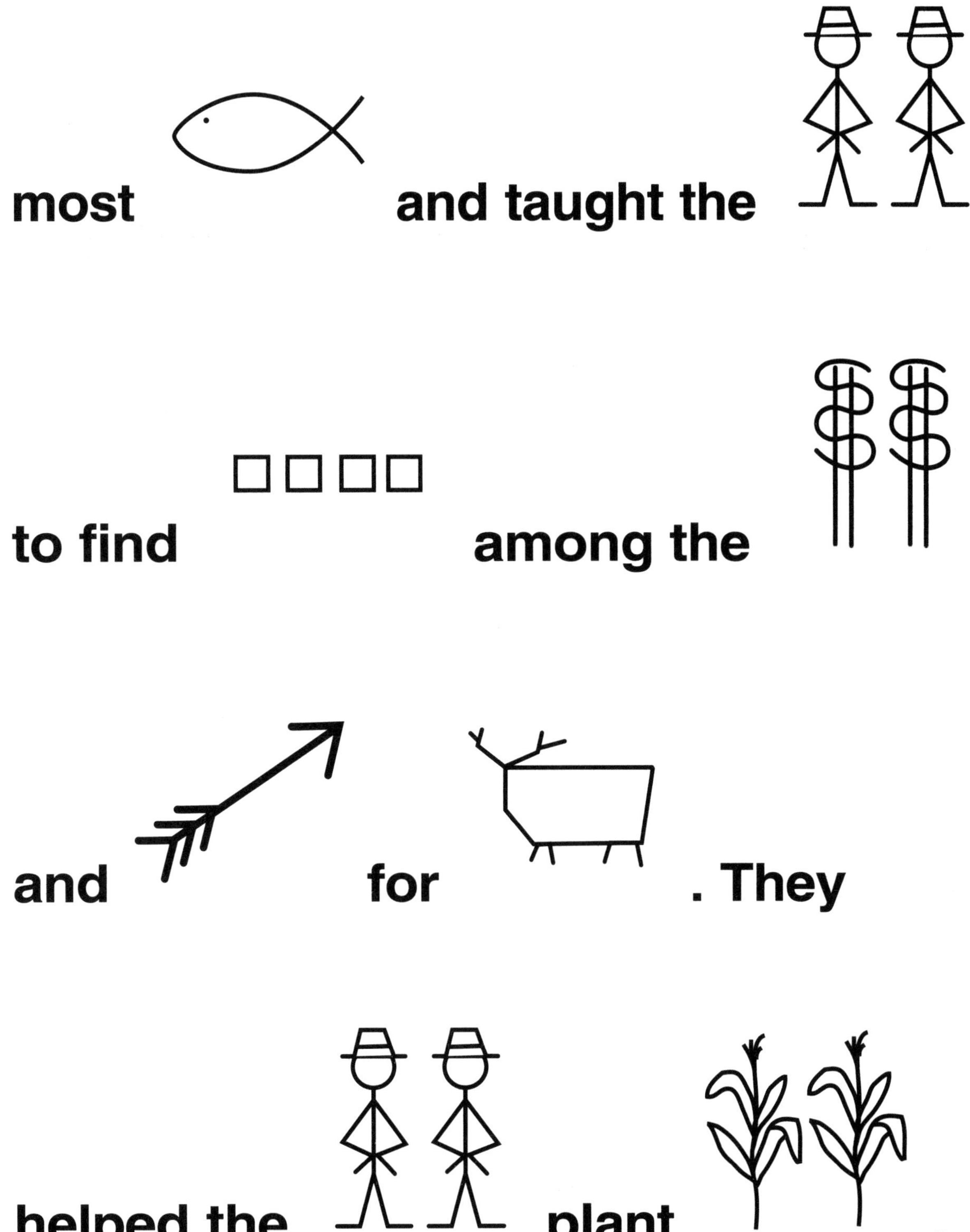
most
and taught the
to find
among the
and
for
. They
helped the
plant
.

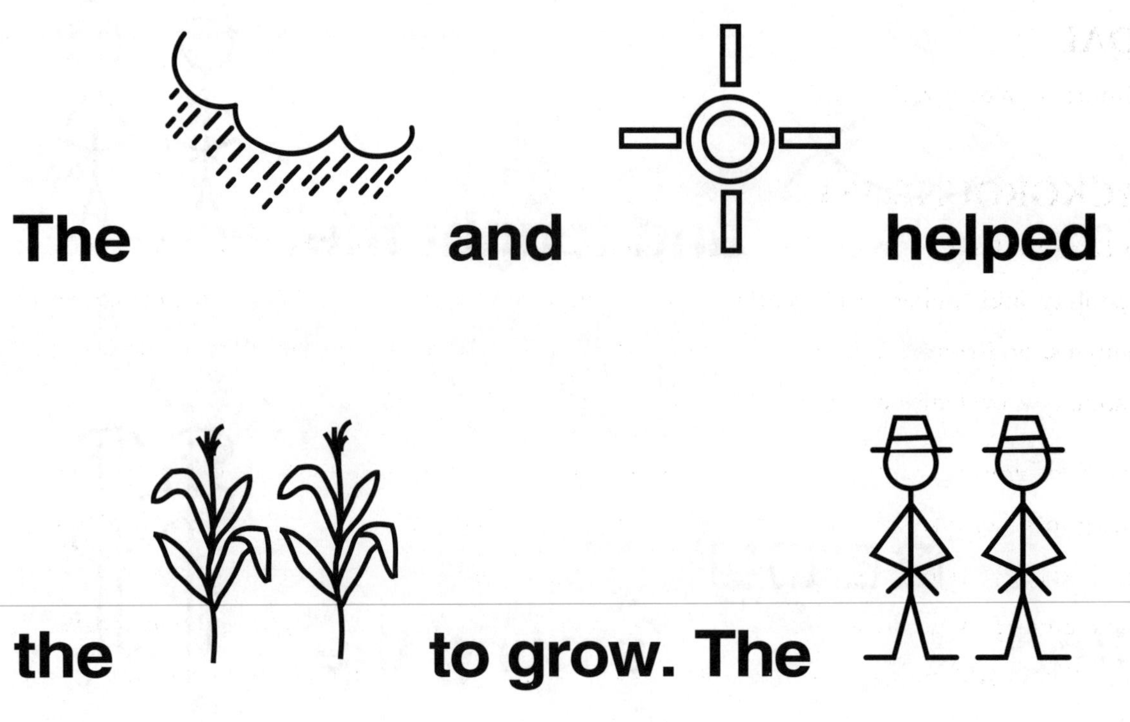

The [rain] and [sun] helped

the [corn] to grow. The [Pilgrims]

were very thankful for their [Native American]

friends. They shared a special [meal].

LASSO THE WORD HERD: CATEGORIES

GOAL

To improve categorization skills

BACKGROUND INFORMATION

The *Lasso the Word Herd: Categories* lesson is one of a series of lessons that help students develop vocabulary and higher level thinking skills, including interpreting symbols, categorizing, using synonyms, and comparing and contrasting. These lessons also work to build "word power" (i.e., vocabulary knowledge and flexibility in word use).

Most of the world around us is organized into various categories. Grocery stores, department stores, parking lots, libraries, and cities are all organized by various attributes. If students understand the organizational systems (i.e., the systems for categorizing) used, they can be more efficient in understanding and using a concept, system, or object. The foundation of categorization is recognizing similarities and differences. This lesson provides opportunities for grouping items, first by discovering similarities and then by comparing similarities and differences.

OBJECTIVES

1. Generate categories by grouping members that are alike.
2. Name categories when given a list of members.

MATERIALS

1. Einstein character (Recommended but not necessary; see page 12.)
2. *Caps, Hats, Socks, and Mittens* (1992), by Louise Borden, illustrated by Lillian Hoban (This book was chosen for its fun depiction of the four seasons and things associated with each. Any book that lists possible members of a category could be used. A book on seasons was chosen to coordinate with the primary curriculum.)
3. Chalkboard and chalk
4. *Lasso the Word Herd* graphic (See page 148; duplicate and enlarge the graphic, color it, mount it onto colorful construction paper or poster board, and laminate it for durability, if desired.)
5. An erasable or water-soluble marker

INTRODUCTION

Tie-in to Prior Learning

Have Einstein remind the students that they used their word power to identify and "read" the special picture symbols used in the last lesson. Have Einstein ask the students what kinds of symbols are especially important at school. Prompt for letter and number symbols. Remind students that reading and interpreting symbols is one of the most important skills they learn in school. Explain that today's lesson focuses on another skill really important at school: categorizing.

Focus/Relevancy

Have Einstein tell the students that his mom hopped onto his lily pad yesterday morning and told him that his pad was a mess! She told him that he needed to get organized and straighten up! Have Einstein discuss with the class how he can sort out the mess (i.e., elicit grouping items by clothing, toys, books, etc.).

LESSON ACTIVITIES

1. Show the students the book *Caps, Hats, Socks, and Mittens,* and highlight the author and the illustrator. Ask the students what they notice about the pictures on the cover. Remind them, if necessary, about the seasonal poems that they read when describing with their sense of touch. Ask them to name the four seasons that are depicted on the cover.

2. Before reading the story, tell the students that their job will be to listen and remember what the characters in the story experience during each season.

3. Explain that when the students group things, as Einstein did in his room with his clothing in one group and his toys in another, they are making categories. (Clap out the syllables several times so the students can practice this long word, *cat/e/gor/ies*). Generate seasonal categories by listing the ideas from the story on the board (e.g., write "Winter Things" and list items or activities below it such as snow, sledding, hot cocoa, mittens, caps, hats).

4. Display the *Lasso the Word Herd* poster that depicts Einstein in western attire holding a lasso. Tell the students that they will be playing a special game called "In Crowd—Out Crowd." Explain the rules:

   Einstein will whisper a category idea to you but will not tell the other students what it is. You need to think of one or two words from this category. Then you'll whisper in my ear and tell me what to write within the lasso on the poster using this special erasable marker. These words will be part of the "in crowd," because they fit in the category. The other students will then guess words that they think are part of the "in crowd" without telling the actual category name. As each word is given, you will decide if the word is part of the "in crowd" or part of the "out crowd." If the word is part of the "in crowd," we'll write it in the lasso circle. If the word is part of the "out crowd," we'll write it outside of the lasso circle. For example, the other students might see the words apple, cherry, strawberry *inside the lasso circle and then guess the word* pear. *If the category is* red *things, we'll put the word* pear *outside the circle. If the category is* fruit, *we'll put the word* pear *inside the circle. As more words are added, either inside or outside the circle, more of you will figure out the secret category. You can demonstrate you know the secret by giving additional words that fit within the category.*

The game continues until no one is giving words that are part of the "out crowd" group or until you ask for someone to share the secret category with the group.

HINT

If the group has a difficult time discerning the category, stop and summarize the information listed inside as well as outside of the lasso circle (e.g., "We know that strawberries, apples, and cherries are in but that pear and lettuce are out"). Point to the items inside the lasso and ask, "How are these things alike? Show me that you know the answer by telling another word that fits the category." Or, if students do not seem to know the category, add more examples within the lasso to help guide the students. Try to keep playing until everyone has figured out the secret. Have a player tell how the words inside the lasso are alike. Encourage them to use wording such as, "They are alike because they are all _____."

5. Play the "In Crowd—Out Crowd" game by using topics that tie in to the curriculum, such as community helpers, round things, triangular things, red things, transportation, colors, seasons, occupations, fruits, vegetables, hot things, or any category ideas that support classroom concepts.

CLOSURE

Summarize the lesson, repeat its relevance to students, and tie it to future learning. Have Einstein say to the students:

By using categories, I could sort and organize the things on my lily pad. You have learned an important tool for organization that can be used at school, at home, or wherever there are things to observe and learn about! In the next lesson, we will learn to organize our words in another useful way.

LASSO THE
WORD HERD!

SAY IT ANOTHER WAY: SYNONYMS

GOAL

To develop vocabulary skills

BACKGROUND INFORMATION

The *Say it Another Way: Synonyms* lesson is one of a series of lessons that help students develop vocabulary and higher level thinking skills, including interpreting symbols, categorizing, using synonyms, and comparing and contrasting. These lessons also work to build "word power" (i.e., vocabulary knowledge and flexibility in word use).

Several objectives are listed since the use of synonyms as a word power tool for improving sentences may be most appropriate for first graders. At the kindergarten level, the educator could elicit synonyms when discussing vocabulary (e.g., when discussing the word *jousting,* which is used in the recommended story, the students may say, "It means 'fighting.'"), but could also focus the lesson on *real* versus *pretend,* or *reality* versus *fantasy,* and drawing conclusions when given a sequence of events or information (see the literary highlights in Activity 2 of the *Lesson Activities* section). At the first-grade level, the students may more formally think about words that have the same meaning and respond to a request to "say it another way." Two separate introductions to the lesson and variations on the lesson have been provided.

OBJECTIVES

1. Give synonyms to clarify sentence meaning.
2. Distinguish between reality and fantasy.
3. Draw conclusions from a given sequence of events.

MATERIALS

1. Einstein character (Recommended but not necessary; see page 12.)
2. *Say It Another Way* graphic (See page 153; duplicate and enlarge the graphic, color it, mount it onto colorful construction paper or poster board, and laminate it for durability, if desired.)
3. *Rocking Horse Christmas* (1997), by Mary Pope Osborne, illustrated by Ned Bittinger (This book was chosen because of the quality of the story and the beautiful illustrations. It lends itself to discussing a variety of adventures that the little boy and his rocking horse encounter on their imaginary trips. The word power concept can be illustrated through the vocabulary that is used throughout the story [e.g., *jousted* for *fought* or *lassoed* for *roped*]. Although this book mentions a

specific holiday, it does not have any particular significance to the story. You may choose another book such as *Sheep Out to Eat,* 1995, by Nancy Shaw, illustrated by Margot Apple, which also uses a wide variety of action verbs [e.g., *dip/scoop, eat/slurp, bite/chomp*] within a fun story.)

INTRODUCTION

Tie-in to Prior Learning

Have Einstein remind the students that they used their word power to discover a secret category by telling how certain items fit into a group. In today's lesson, we'll make more word groups.

Focus/Relevancy

NOTE: Depending on the level of the students, two separate *focus/relevancy* ideas are presented.

1. Real—Pretend

   Have Einstein ask the students if they have heard the story or seen the movie *101 Dalmatians.* (Any well-known story or movie can be used as an example.) Then have him ask the students if they think the story is real or pretend and discuss their reasons why. The discussion might include ideas that could be true and ideas that would have to be pretend, or fantasy. Show the *Say It Another Way* poster, and have the students identify and explain what could be real and what could only be pretend in the illustrations. Have Einstein tell the students that today they will be listening to a special story that will have parts that might be real and parts that might be pretend. Their job will be to listen for these different parts and to categorize them.

2. Synonyms: "Say it a different way."

   Einstein tells the students that he is writing a story at school about a wonderful feast his family and friends shared at the pond. He is feeling a little frustrated because he wants his listeners to know how delicious the food tasted and how much fun he had playing, but his ideas seem a little boring. Professor Green told him he has the word power to make his story more exciting by learning to say his ideas in a different way. Einstein discovered he could use words like *gobbled, nibbled,* and *chomped* to describe how his cousins *ate* their juicy beetle casserole. Show the *Say It Another Way* poster, and then place it on the board. Explain that Einstein can tell about the same event in different ways by using more interesting words (e.g., when telling about *jumping* from one beanstalk to another, he could be *hopping, bounding,* or *leaping).*

LESSON ACTIVITIES

1. Show the cover of the book *Rocking Horse Christmas*. Have the students predict what they think the story might be about. Explain that as they listen to the story, they will be thinking about (a) real versus pretend events or (b) telling what certain words mean and then saying them "a different way."

2. Read the story. Highlight the following literary components, as appropriate:

   - Real—Pretend

   Discuss: The author says, "They took off." Where might they go? Was this real or pretend? Why?

   Summarize: For each adventure, have the students tell where the boy and his horse really are and explain where they are pretending to be. Study the clues in the pictures. Adventures include visiting the wild west, jousting with knights, building a stall, going on an African safari, racing in the Kentucky Derby, and fighting a Tyrannosaurus rex. Elicit the concepts of past, present, long ago, etc.

   - Vocabulary: *lassoed, West/East, jousted, knights, stall, safari, plain, derby, mane, attic, frail, blizzard, fade, hatch, streamed, jump, dawn*

   - Synonyms: *under/below, lassoed/roped, jousted/fought, mane/hair, derby/race, blizzard/storm, leap/jump, dawn/morning*

3. Have students draw conclusions, inferences, and predictions.

   - Why did the bear and rocking horse feel sad when they looked out the bedroom window?
   - Why was the rocking horse taken to the attic?
   - Where was Shadow's boy? Who did the rocking horse see riding a bicycle and visiting with a woman and a baby?
   - How did the window get broken?
   - Who is the man?
   - Who is the new boy?

4. Summarize the concept of real versus pretend or the concept "Say it a different way." Ask, "What was real about the rocking horse story? What was pretend?" Or ask, "Why did the author use different words that mean the same thing, for example, *jousted* instead of *fought*?"

CLOSURE

Summarize the lesson, repeat its relevance to students, and tie it to future learning. Have Einstein compliment both the author and the illustrator on their use of wonderful pictures and words to tell an exciting story. This author really used her word power! Tell the students that in the next lesson, they will be using *their* word power to tell how things are alike and different.

SAY IT ANOTHER WAY

ALIKE AND DIFFERENT LILY PADS (PART I)

GOAL

To compare and contrast information

BACKGROUND INFORMATION

The *Alike and Different Lily Pads* lesson is one of a series of lessons that help students develop vocabulary and higher level thinking skills, including interpreting symbols, categorizing, using synonyms, and comparing and contrasting. These lessons also work to build "word power" (i.e., vocabulary knowledge and flexibility in word use).

OBJECTIVES

1. Understand and use the terms *alike* and *different* or *compare* and *contrast*, to tell how things are alike and different.
2. Compare and contrast animals, stories, places, or events.

MATERIALS

1. Einstein character (Recommended but not necessary; see page 12.)
2. *Who Is the Beast?* (1990), by Keith Baker (This book was selected because it shows how a group of seemingly different animals also share some similar characteristics. It also lends itself to a discussion about feelings and being sensitive to others.)
3. *Alike and Different Lily Pads* graphic (See page 157; duplicate and enlarge the graphic, color it, mount it onto colorful construction paper or poster board, and laminate it for durability, if desired.)
4. An erasable or water-soluble marker

INTRODUCTION

Tie-in to Prior Learning

Have Einstein remind the students about how they have continued to build word power by learning words that can be used in different ways. In the last lesson, they listened to a story that used some special words. Einstein can ask the students if they remember what the word *joust* means, or another word for *lassoed*. He can remind the students that when they use more powerful words, it makes their ideas more interesting. In the last lesson, the students also had to listen and watch for clues to distinguish events that could really happen from those events that were in the little boy's imagination.

Focus/Relevancy

Have Einstein tell about some of his friends at the pond. He can tell that many of his friends are green, bumpy, and croak, but he also has a friend that is big, white, and quacks. All of his friends enjoy a good swim in the pond. Ask, "What is it?" (a duck). Have Einstein tell the students that today they will be learning about some other animals that appear to be very different.

LESSON ACTIVITIES

1. Ask the students what the word *beast* means. Let a number of students share their ideas. Show the cover of the book *Who Is the Beast?* by Keith Baker. Ask the students who they think the beast will be in the book.

2. Read the book. Highlight the following literary components as the story is read:

   - Opposite words: *low/high, left/right*

   - Synonyms: *sure/strong, far/long*

   - Rhyming words: The educator may want to let students predict the rhyming words as used within the story.

   - Multiple meaning words: *fly, back, tracks*

   The illustrations are wonderful and students have to discover which creature is talking on each page. As the story progresses, the author highlights similarities between the different animals and the tiger. Discuss the feelings depicted on the tiger's face in different parts of the story. The author begins the story by pointing out certain features that a particular animal fears (e.g., "The beast, the beast... I see his whiskers long and white."). Later in the story, the author compares the tiger's long whiskers to those on the catfish and points out how each animal has a feature that can be compared to those of the tiger.

3. To illustrate comparing or telling how things are alike, show the *Alike and Different Lily Pads* poster (a Venn diagram made from lily pads) and write *tiger* on one side and another animal on the other (e.g., *catfish*). Ask the students if there is a way that a tiger is the same as, or like, a catfish. Elicit visual information, such as "Both have whiskers" or categorical information, such as "Both are animals." Write this information in the middle of the Venn diagram. Point out that since both animals share this trait, it is written in the space shared by both lily pads. Explain that by finding ways a tiger and a catfish are alike, the students have compared the two animals.

4. To illustrate contrasting, or telling how things are different, show the *Alike and Different Lily Pads* poster and list ideas such as "Fish live under water" or "Tigers live on land." Point out that the catfish trait will be listed on the catfish side of the lily pad diagram since the tiger does not share this particular trait. Follow with the tiger trait on the tiger side of the diagram. Model a summary of the information on the *Alike and Different Lily Pads* poster for the students (e.g., "A tiger and a catfish are alike because they are both animals with whiskers; but they are different because a catfish lives under the water and a tiger lives on land").

   HINT
   The students may be able to tell many differences, but you may want to limit the number listed so that other animals may be contrasted.

5. Continue with the other animals as time permits. Have different students come up to the chart to summarize, or make the summary a group activity with all the students summarizing chorally as you point to the ideas.

   HINT
   You will have to gauge the reading skills of the group at this point in the year. Students may benefit from stick-figure symbols added quickly to help them "read" along (e.g., after writing "They both have whiskers," you might draw a smiley face with whiskers or draw whiskers around the word *whiskers*).

CLOSURE

Summarize the lesson, repeat its relevance to students, and tie it to future learning. Have Einstein review comparing and contrasting by reminding the students about his friends at the pond. He can tell the students that his friends are alike because they all like to swim; but they are different because his frog friends are green, bumpy, and croak, while his duck friend is big, white, and quacks. Tell the students that in the next lesson, they will have another opportunity to compare and contrast by telling how two stories can be alike and different at the same time.

Alike and Different Lily Pads

ALIKE AND DIFFERENT LILY PADS (PART II)

GOAL

To compare and contrast information

BACKGROUND INFORMATION

The *Alike and Different Lily Pads* lesson is part of a series of lessons that help students develop vocabulary and higher level thinking skills, including interpreting symbols, categorizing, using synonyms, and comparing and contrasting. These lessons also work to build "word power" (i.e., vocabulary knowledge and flexibility in word use).

In Part I, the students were exposed to a Venn diagram in the shape of lily pads to compare and contrast animals or objects. Part II takes the concept to a more difficult level, since the students compare and contrast two whole stories.

OBJECTIVES

1. Understand and use the terms *alike* and *different* or *compare* and *contrast*, to tell how things are alike and different.
2. Compare and contrast animals, stories, places, or events.

MATERIALS

1. Einstein character (Recommended but not necessary; see page 12.)
2. *The Three Little Javelinas* (1992), by Susan Lowell, illustrated by Jim Harris (This book was selected because it gives a fun, different slant to a familiar story. This story takes place in a desert region and could be compared to the students' particular regional area.)
3. *Alike and Different Lily Pads* poster (Created earlier)
4. An erasable or water-soluble marker

INTRODUCTION

Tie-in to Prior Learning

Have Einstein remind the students that in the last lesson, they discovered that a tiger can be compared to a catfish. Ask the students to tell how a tiger is like a catfish.

Focus/Relevancy

Have Einstein call on two students to come to the front of the room. Ask the class to compare the two students by telling ways they are alike. Show the *Alike and Different Lily Pads* poster, and ask the students where to put the information that is the same. Fill in several likenesses. Now ask the students to contrast the pair by telling ways they are different. Once again, ask where to write the information that shows differences and fill in the diagram. Einstein can tell the students that in today's lesson, they will be using their word power by comparing and contrasting two whole stories.

LESSON ACTIVITIES

1. Show the cover of the story *The Three Little Javelinas,* and read the title to the class. Ask the students if this book reminds them of any other story. Lead the students to relate this story to *The Three Little Pigs*. Tell the students to listen for ways the *The Three Little Javelinas* story is alike and different from the *The Three Little Pigs* story.

2. Highlight the following literary components *before* the story is read:

   - Tell the students that this story is about a special kind of pig called a *javelina* (ha-ve-LEE-na), which means "wild hog."

   - Ask the students to look at the javelinas on the front cover and to compare and contrast them to pigs.

   - Ask where the story is taking place. Talk about what they notice about a desert region.

   Begin reading the story. Highlight the following literary components as the story is read:

   - Key vocabulary: *snout, whirlwind, tumbleweed, coyote, saguaro* (suh-GWAR-o) *cactus, suspicious, chaps* (not specifically mentioned, but they are pictured), *Ha'u* and *sí* ("yes"), *adobe bricks, budge, cackle*

   - Figurative language: *hullabaloo, smooth as oil*

3. Using the *Alike and Different Lily Pads* poster to capture ideas, let students tell ways that the two stories are alike and different. As information is added, you can periodically summarize the information by saying, "The stories are alike because…" or "The stories are different because…"

CLOSURE

Summarize the lesson, repeat its relevance to students, and tie it to future learning. Review comparing and contrasting by having the students "read" the information from the poster together (i.e., "The stories are alike because… They are different because…"). Tell the students that in the next lesson, they will have an opportunity to show off their word power!

STRATEGY REVIEW LESSON 3

GOAL

To reinforce and review the strategies for "word power" (i.e., vocabulary knowledge and flexibility in word use) and higher level thinking skills

BACKGROUND INFORMATION

The main focus of this lesson is to review the strategies for word power and higher level thinking skills: *Symbols Have Meaning, Lasso the Word Herd: Categories, Say It Another Way: Synonyms,* and *Alike and Different Lily Pads.* A review lesson is provided after several strategies have been taught. In addition, the students take home *Homework Activity* pages and *Communication Skills Newsletter No. 3* to encourage family involvement and understanding of the language skills.

OBJECTIVES

1. Review and practice the major components of the *Symbols Have Meaning, Lasso the Word Herd: Categories, Say It Another Way: Synonyms,* and *Alike and Different Lily Pads* strategies.
2. Complete the application activities.
3. Share strategy information with family members.

MATERIALS

1. Einstein character (Recommended but not necessary; see page 12.)
2. *Symbols Have Meaning* poster (Created earlier)
3. *Lasso the Word Herd* poster (Created earlier)
4. *Say It Another Way* poster (Created earlier)
5. *Alike and Different Lily Pads* poster (Created earlier)
6. *Homework Activity* pages (See pages 162–165; duplicate for each student.)
7. *Skills Checklist* (See page 166; duplicate and enlarge the checklist, copy it, mount it onto colorful construction paper or poster board, and laminate it, if desired.)
8. *Communication Skills Newsletter No. 3* (See pages 167–168; duplicate for each student.)

INTRODUCTION

Tie-in to Prior Learning

Einstein can remind the students that they have been learning many important skills to help them develop word power. Display and briefly review the posters and strategies for these lessons.

Focus/Relevancy

Einstein can remind the students about the last time they had homework, and compliment the students on what a good job they did teaching their families about word power. He can tell them that they are going to have another special homework assignment, to be worked on with an older family member. Tell the students that their families will be really impressed when they hear how much they have learned!

LESSON ACTIVITIES

1. Briefly show the students the *Homework Activity* pages and relate the questions on the sheets to the posters *(Symbols Have Meaning, Lasso the Word Herd, Say It Another Way,* and *Alike and Different Lily Pads)* on the board.
2. Have Einstein select several students to model answers for the class, or have the entire class give choral responses to review questions from the *Homework Activity* pages.
3. Display the *Skills Checklist.* Review the key components of a lesson while looking at the poster and by practicing some items from the *Homework Activity* pages. Place or have students place a checkmark on the line beside each skill as the review is completed.
4. Show the students *Communication Skills Newsletter No. 3.* Explain that even their parents have homework. The newsletter describes the activities that they have been doing in class.
5. Hand out the *Homework Activity* pages and *Communication Skills Newsletter No. 3* for the students to take home, or place them in envelopes for students to take home.

CLOSURE

Summarize the lesson, repeat its relevance to students, and tie it to future learning. Have Einstein encourage the students to share their *Homework Activity* pages and *Communication Skills Newsletter No. 3* with someone special at home. Explain that after they have completed the homework, they should have their parent or caregiver sign and date in the appropriate space and return it for a reward (e.g., a sticker or points on a homework chart). Congratulate the students on their growing use of word power. Tell the students that in the next lesson, they will get to practice telling opposite words.

Homework Activity

Name: ______________________________

1. Tell your parents what these symbols mean:

a.

b.

c.

2. Draw a picture symbol for each word.

cat **happy**

3. Write a number symbol for:

______________________ **apples**

Family Member: ______________________ Date: ______________

Homework Activity

Name: ______________________________

1. **Tell another word for each of the following:**

   a. large　　b. quick

   c. forest　　d. hop

2. **Tell about a real day at school.**
   Tell something pretend that could happen.

3. **Think about these ideas.**
   Are they real or pretend?

   - I built a shopping center in my bedroom.
   - We saw an elephant on our safari!
   - A dinosaur came to our school.
   - We saw a puppet show.

Family Member: ______________________ Date: ______________

Homework Activity

Name: ______________________________

Words have been "lassoed" into a group. Write two more words that fit in the lasso. Then complete the sentence "They are all ________."

They are all ________________.

They are all ________________.

They are all ________________.

Family Member: ______________________ Date: ______________

Homework Activity

Name: ______________________________

Comparing is looking at how things are alike.

Contrasting is looking at how things are different.

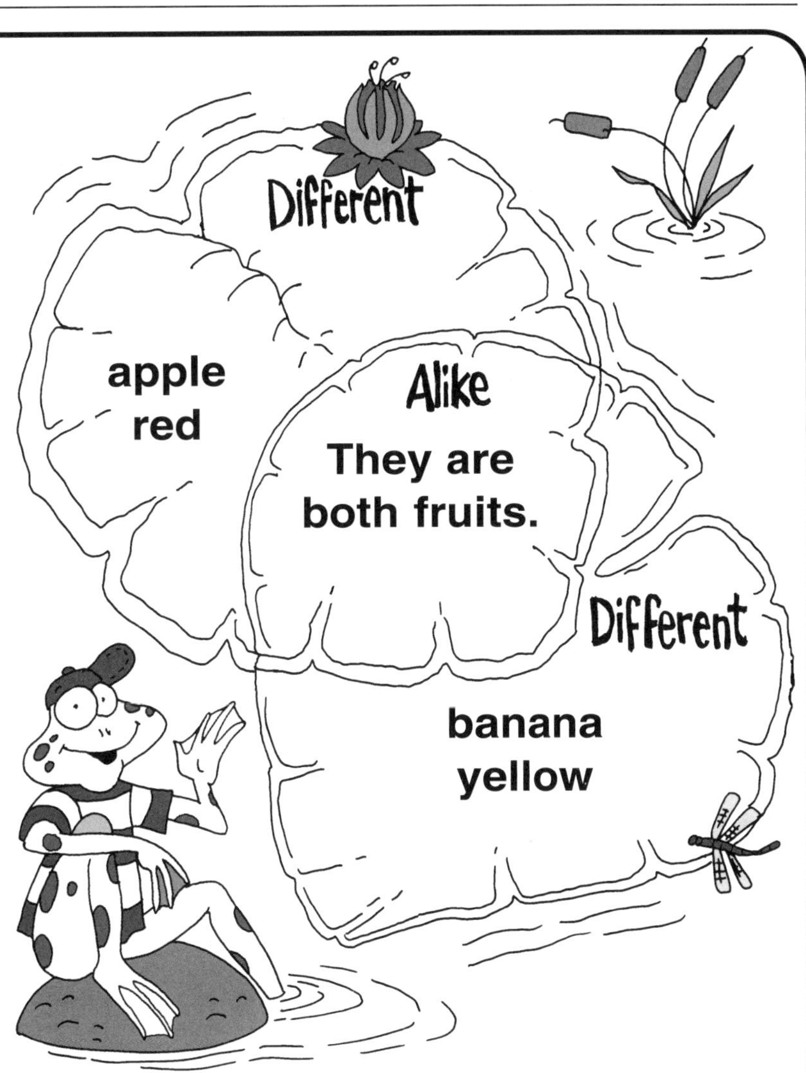

Tell how these words are alike and different:

1. potato chip and apple
2. tiger and bumble bee
3. crayon and pencil

Family Member: ______________________ Date: ______________

Skills Checklist

Skill ✓Up

In the last unit, I worked on…

1. Symbols:
I can *draw* or *write* my words. ________

2. Categories:
I can tell which group something fits into! "A cow is a kind of ________." ________

3. Synonyms: "I can say it another way" with synonyms. I can tell another word for *jump, big,* and *jog.* I can also tell how *real* and *pretend* are different. ________

4. Compare and Contrast: ________
I can tell how things are *alike* and *different.*

Communication Skills Newsletter

No. 3

Word Power!

We have been working hard since our lessons on describing with our five senses. We have developed more "word power" by practicing a variety of new language skills, while still continuing to use our active listening and senses to discover and describe our world. This newsletter will tell you about our word power.

The Power of Symbols

We talked about the use of *symbols* to represent words, ideas, or objects. Some of the symbols that we discussed were the flag, letters, and numbers. We saw how pictures symbols could be used to tell about events that happened a long time ago. The students predicted picture symbol meanings for a story about Pilgrims first coming to America. We discussed why certain pictures were used to represent an ocean, a river, a lake, tall trees, deer, tracks, food, rain, a feast, and friends.

We learned communication can take a variety of forms, including words, letters, numbers, pictures, and gestures. The students were encouraged to record their own important events, such as holidays, birthdays, etc., in whatever format is most useful to them.

The Power of Categories

We practiced recognizing how objects might fit together within a group or category, (e.g., all colors, all fruits, all vegetables).

We used a picture of Einstein dressed as a cowboy and his lasso. We played a special game called "In Crowd—Out Crowd" to figure out secret categories. In this game, the person who is "it" writes one or two words inside the lasso (e.g., *apple, strawberry*). The other players have to figure out what the secret category is by guessing words that they think might fit inside the lasso, without telling the secret! If the secret category is "things that are red" and a player guesses "banana," it would be written outside of the lasso. If the secret category is "fruit," then "banana" would be written inside the lasso. The person who was "it" would then call on a player to tell the secret (e.g., "They are all *things that are red*").

This is a fun game to play with your child at home too!

The Power of Saying Something Another Way

We strengthened our word power by thinking about how some words can mean the same thing. We can "say it another way" if we know both of the meanings. We read the book *Rocking Horse Christmas*, by Mary Pope Osborne, and learned that reading is a fun way to learn new words! These words included *under/below, lassoed/roped, jousted/fought, stared/looked, leap/jump, gallop/run.* Ask your child to tell you another way to say tiny (little), large (big). This helps to develop flexibility in language use. In this lesson, the students also identified the adventures in the story that could be *real* and those that were *pretend*. The students looked for clues within the story to support their answer.

What We're Going to Do Next

Einstein and Professor Green will be teaching even more word power skills to use in the next few weeks. We're going to learn about opposites next. After that, we're going to talk about words that are related to each other like "bike/ride" and "jacket/zipper." Keep talking at home about word power!

The Power of Describing Likenesses and Differences

Our most recent skill was *comparing* and *contrasting* or telling how things are *alike* and *different*. The children are proud of the fact that they can compare and contrast two objects. They were encouraged to use sentences to tell how objects are alike and different. We read the book *Who Is the Beast?* by Keith Baker, which describes how a tiger in the jungle shares features with other animals. We used these ideas to practice comparing and contrasting (e.g., a tiger and a catfish are alike because they both have whiskers and are animals; but they are different because a tiger stays on dry land and a catfish swims in the water).

We also used our *alike and different* strategy to compare two different versions of a familiar fairy tale. We read the story, *The Three Little Javalinas*, by Susan Lowell. We talked about how that story and *The Three Little Pigs* are alike and different. This is an important academic skill, since students will often be called upon to compare stories, events, objects, famous people, etc.

LEARNING ABOUT OPPOSITES

GOAL

To develop vocabulary skills

BACKGROUND INFORMATION

The *Learning about Opposites* lesson is one of a series of lessons that help students develop vocabulary and higher level thinking skills, including naming antonyms, solving analogies, and defining objects clearly. These lessons also work to build "word power" (i.e., vocabulary knowledge and flexibility in word use).

In this lesson, students focus on word pairs that are opposites. They will need to use their previously learned listening skills while catching "errors" in words used by the educator. The errors consist of the educator purposefully substituting the opposite word for the one intended. The students' job is to identify the errors.

OBJECTIVES

1. Understand the concept of opposite.
2. Generate antonyms.
3. Recognize when an opposite is needed to correct a sentence that doesn't make sense.

MATERIALS

1. Einstein character (Recommended but not necessary; see page 12.)
2. *Use Opposite Words* graphic (See page 172; duplicate and enlarge the graphic, color it, mount it onto colorful construction paper or poster board, and laminate it for durability, if desired.)
3. *That's Good! That's Bad!* (1993), by Margery Cuyler, illustrated by David Catrow (This book was selected because of the entertaining illustrations and easy adaptability for a lesson on opposite words. Any story with many concept words that lend themselves to generating opposites could be used, such as *Dinner at the Panda Palace,* 1995, by Stephanie Calmenson, illustrated by Nadine Bernard Westcott.)
4. Small sticky notes with opposite words written on them: *shiny/dull, high/low, hot/cold, tall/short, little/big, noisy/quiet, play/work, big/little, lost/found, back/front, up/down, stop/go, asleep/awake, daddy/ mommy, night/day, dark/light, cry/laugh, afraid/brave, never/ always*

INTRODUCTION

Tie-in to Prior Learning

Have Einstein remind the students that they used their word power to "say it another way" with synonyms, or words with the same meaning. Now they can use exciting words to tell about stories and events that they experience. Instead of using a "plain" word, such as *run,* they can use a better word, such as *dash, race,* or *speed.*

Focus/Relevancy

Have Einstein tell about the big day on the pond when a herd of thirsty elephants came and slurped up most of the water in the pond! The water was not high but low, and the fish were all cramped into a puddle! Have him ask the students if they think that was good or bad and to explain why. (The students will most likely think this is a tragic event and may have a variety of reasons why.) Have Einstein point out that rather than a bad situation, it was the opposite. It turned out to be a good turn of events, because it rained and rained for days after the elephants left and the pond filled up with fresh, clear water for the happy fish. Show the *Use Opposite Words* poster, and explain that in today's lesson, the students will be learning about *good, bad,* and a variety of other opposite words to help them be smart thinkers. If they can remember opposites, they can keep from being tricked or making a mistake, as well as learn new words! There are many opposite words that they will learn as they grow older. Have Einstein lead them in telling some simple opposites by saying, "The opposite of up is..." (down) "The opposite of high is..." (low) "The opposite of hot is..." (cold). (You may use hand or body gestures that the students can follow to help visually illustrate the opposite. For example, when saying *high,* stretch your arms up, and when saying *low,* stretch them downward. When saying *hot,* fan yourself with your hands, and when saying *cold,* pretend to shiver.)

LESSON ACTIVITIES

1. Show the cover of the book *That's Good! That's Bad!* Introduce the author and illustrator. Ask the students to predict what they think the story is about. Explain that as the story is read, their listening job will be to "catch" the teacher if he or she reads the opposite of what makes sense in the story. Give examples of what they might hear, such as "We eat breakfast at night" or "We stand in our chair." Allow the students to identify and correct the questionable word.

2. The author uses the phrases "Oh, that's good! No, that's bad!" or "Oh, that's bad! No, that's good!" after each outrageous event in the story. Have the students explain whether or not a situation is good or bad by guessing or predicting what will happen next (e.g., the boy floats up in the air while hanging on to a balloon string, and the balloon is popped by a tall prickly tree

in a jungle. The students will read along with the educator and say, "Oh, that's bad!" but then the educator will say, "No, that's good!" The students will then predict why that could end up being a good situation.)

3. Insert the sticky notes on the appropriate pages in *That's Good! That's Bad!* Read the "trick" word in place of the actual word in the text. Help students pick out the error, and reread it the correct way.

HINT
A fun aspect of this story is the sound words or exclamations included on each page (i.e., Wow! Pop! Splat! Giddyap! Whee! SSSSsssss! Whoops! Hooray! Glug, Glug; Whoosh! ZZZZZzzz! Slurp! Yuck! BooHoo! Whish! Sob! Great!). Have the students read these from a chart, or have them written ahead of time on the board. The students can look and listen to the story and follow along with the list of words. Point out the appropriate sound word as the story is read, and have the students help to make the sound effect. Read through the list with the students before reading the story.

CLOSURE

Summarize the lesson, repeat its relevance to students, and tie it to future learning. Have Einstein compliment the students on how well they "caught" the teacher's tricks and used opposite words to correct the story. Explain that in the next lesson, they will be using all of their word power skills to solve special word puzzles!

Use Opposite Words
to Build
WORD
POWER
high
big
little
off
on
low

DISCOVER THE PATTERN: MAKING CONNECTIONS (PART I)

GOAL

To improve expressive language skills by solving analogies

BACKGROUND INFORMATION

The *Discover the Pattern: Making Connections* lesson is one of a series of lessons that help students develop vocabulary and higher level thinking skills, including naming antonyms, solving analogies, and defining objects clearly. These lessons also work to build "word power" (i.e., vocabulary knowledge and flexibility in word use).

Part I of this lesson has students apply what they know about vocabulary words and their word power to discover the pattern or relationship necessary to solve simple analogies (e.g., synonyms, antonyms, item/category, item/feature, part/whole, item/function, and item/location). Solving analogies requires knowledge of vocabulary and flexibility in using the words they know. This strategy also relies on students' knowledge of categorization to recognize relationships in analogies.

OBJECTIVES

1. Identify the pattern in an analogy.
2. Solve an analogy using pictures and words.

MATERIALS

1. Einstein character (Recommended but not necessary; see page 12.)
2. *Pattern Pictures* (See pages 176–177; duplicate and enlarge the pictures; color them using a predictable pattern according to *focus/relevancy* directions, and laminate them for durability, if desired.)
3. *Discover the Pattern* graphic (See page 178; duplicate and enlarge the graphic, color it, mount it onto colorful construction paper or poster board, and laminate it for durability, if desired.)
4. *Pattern Relationships* graphics (See pages 179–185; duplicate and enlarge the graphics, color them, mount them onto colorful construction paper or poster board, and laminate them for durability, if desired.)
5. Chalkboard or magnetic board
6. *Pattern Cards* (See pages 186–192; duplicate them onto heavy stock paper, color them, and cut them apart to form cards.)

INTRODUCTION

Tie-in to Prior Learning

Have Einstein remind the students that in the last lesson, they had to listen carefully to the story *That's Good! That's Bad!* to keep from getting "tricked" whenever the educator read the wrong opposite word. Ask the students to use a whisper voice to tell what we call words like *good/bad, up/down,* or *hot/cold.* Einstein can ask the students what they have been "building" over the last few months. Elicit the concept of word power. Tell the students that they will be using all their word power skills in today's lesson.

Focus/Relevancy

1. Einstein can tell the students that he noticed something unusual about some flowers that had been planted by the pond. He saw a yellow tulip, a red tulip, and a white daisy, and then a yellow tulip, a red tulip, and a white daisy again. Have Einstein show a picture of the flowers and ask the students what they notice about the colors (see page 176). Have Einstein ask the students which color flowers would come next. Ask the students how they were able to predict the answers. Elicit the idea of recognizing the pattern. Then Einstein can show a picture of a row of clouds (see page 177), which follow a shape pattern. Discuss their predictions of which clouds would come next.

   Have Einstein tell the students that words can follow patterns too, and that in today's lesson, they will be using their word power to discover these patterns.

2. Show the *Discover the Pattern* poster. Ask if anyone can complete the pattern. Point out that possible answers are given on the poster. Have students make guesses and explain their answers. Help students see that the large triangle comes next because that's the pattern. Tell them that in this lesson, they will be learning how to discover the pattern to solve the word puzzle.

LESSON ACTIVITIES

1. The analogies in this lesson are based on patterns or relationships representing synonyms, antonyms, item/category, item/feature, part/whole, item/function, and item/location. These relationships are illustrated on the *Pattern Relationships* posters (see pages 179–185).

2. Show a pattern example (e.g., big:large), which is taken from one of the seven *Pattern Relationships* posters. Model and practice how the pattern is read (e.g., say, "Big **goes with** large **as** small **goes with** little").

3. Place a *Pattern Card* example for each relationship on the board using tape or a magnet. Give each child one part of a *Pattern Card* set. Have students come up one at a time to match their

pattern with the appropriate relationship (i.e., if the example for location shows *nest:tree,* the students would match other location examples, such as *car:garage* or *frog:pond*). You may want to model reading the examples as a complete analogy statement.

NOTE: There are a number of examples for each relationship that will match the original pattern, so every child has an opportunity to take a turn.

CLOSURE

Summarize the lesson, repeat its relevance to students, and tie it to future learning. Review the relationship patterns that the students created emphasizing critical information (e.g., "These cards make a pattern because they all tell locations"). Compliment the students on their use of word power to discover the patterns. Tell the students that in Part II of this lesson, they will be discovering some new patterns that use letters and sounds in words.

Pattern Pictures

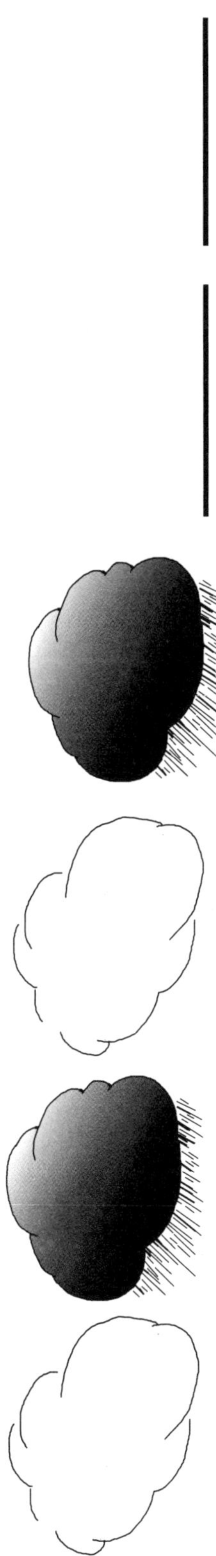

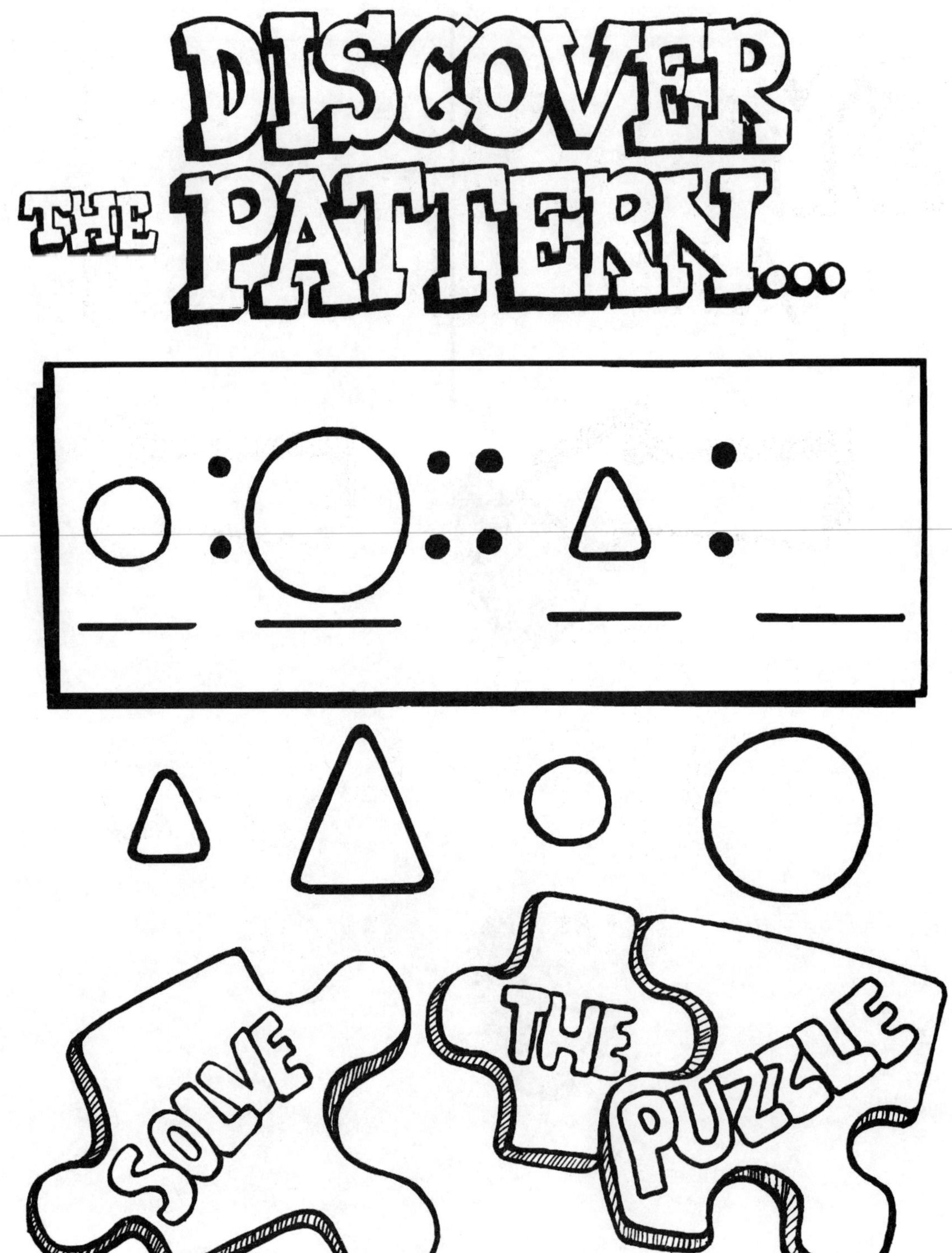
DISCOVER
THE PATTERN...
SOLVE
THE
PUZZLE

Pattern Relationships

SYNONYMS ARE THE SAME

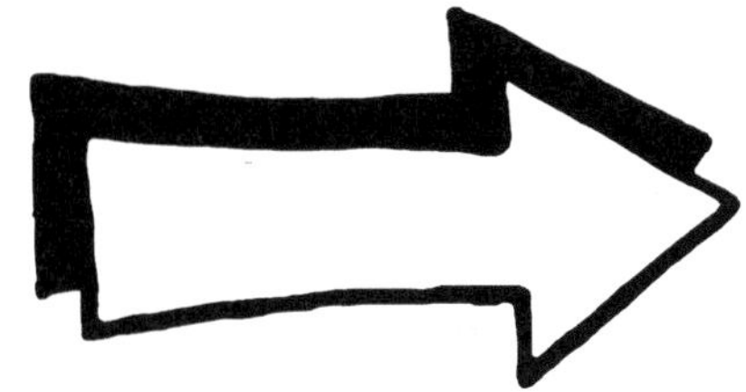

big : large

small : little

ANTONYMS
ARE OPPOSITES

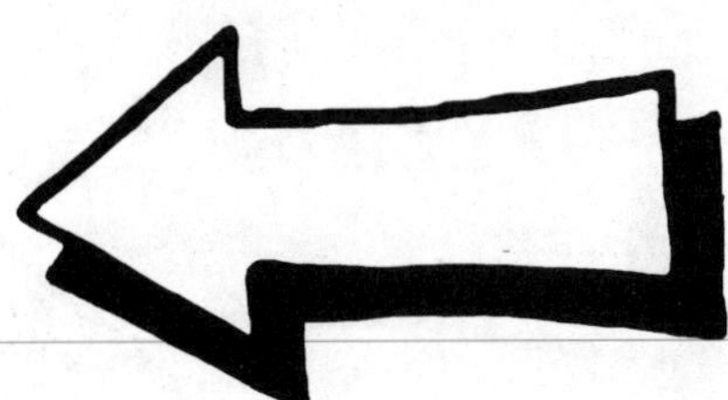
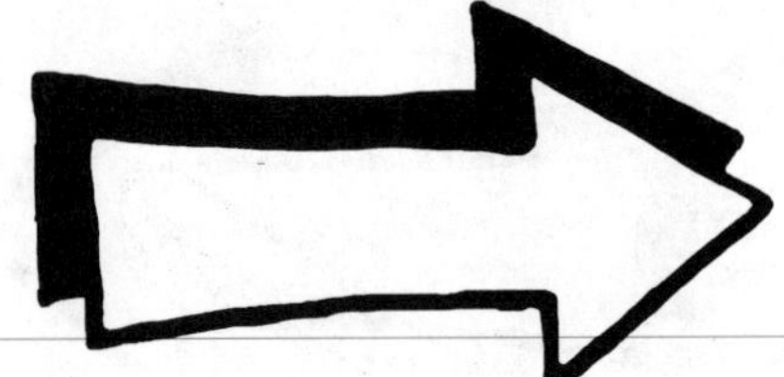

big : little

small : large

Item/Category

bird : animals

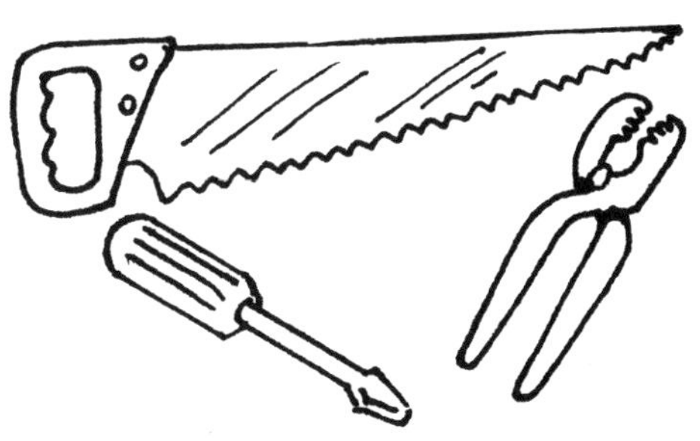

hammer : tools

car : vehicles

Item/Feature

: small

: prickly

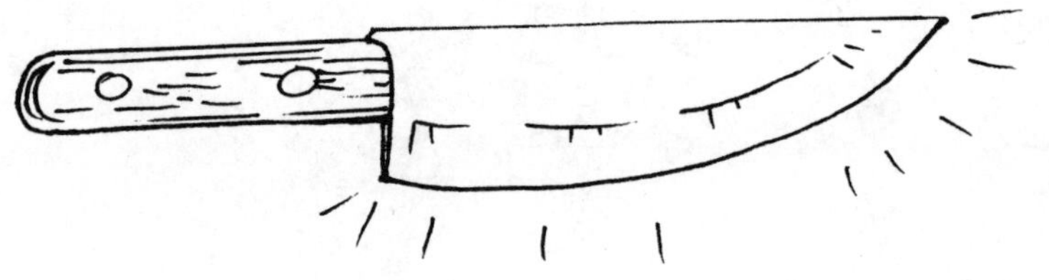

: sharp

Part/Whole

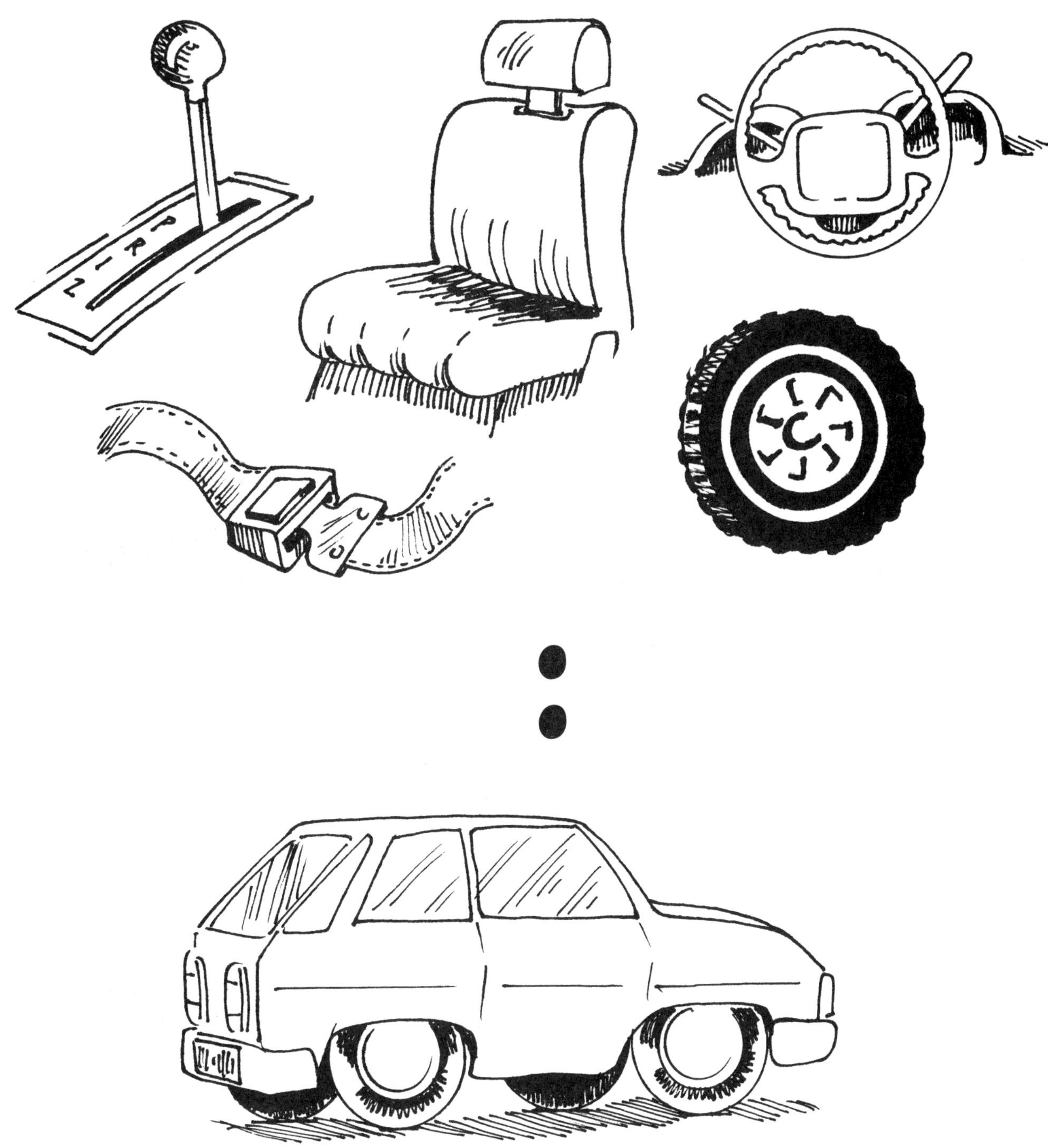

Item/Function

knife : cuts

pencil : writes

horn : honks

Item/Location

food refrigerator

Pattern Cards: Antonyms

Pattern Cards: Functions

Pattern Cards: Features

Pattern Cards: Categories

Pattern Cards: Synonyms

Pattern Cards: Locations

Pattern Cards: Parts of a Whole

DISCOVER THE PATTERN: MAKING CONNECTIONS (PART II)

GOAL

To improve expressive language skills by recognizing and generating rhyming words

BACKGROUND INFORMATION

The *Discover the Pattern: Making Connections* lesson is one of a series of lessons that help students develop vocabulary and higher level thinking skills, including naming antonyms, solving analogies, and defining objects clearly. These lessons also work to build "word power" (i.e., vocabulary knowledge and flexibility in word use).

Part II of this lesson has students apply what they know about patterns to develop phonological awareness as it pertains to identifying rhyming words both visually and auditorally. Phonological awareness is an important school skill in that it helps students develop discrimination skills and sound-symbol relationships, which are prerequisite to learning new vocabulary and written language.

OBJECTIVES

1. Identify the pattern of simple rhyming words when only the beginning sounds change.
2. Generate rhyming words using both visual and auditory cues.

MATERIALS

1. Einstein character (Recommended but not necessary; see page 12.)
2. Chalkboard and chalk
3. *Rhyming Word Patterns* (From *Each Peach Pear Plum;* see page 195; duplicate and enlarge the page, mount it onto colorful construction paper or poster board, and laminate it for durability, if desired.)
4. *Each Peach Pear Plum* (1979), by Janet and Allan Ahlberg (This book was selected because it provides predictable opportunities to generate rhyming words. In addition, the students enjoy "spying" the featured character on each page. Any books that use rhyming words could be substituted.)

INTRODUCTION

Tie-in to Prior Learning

Have Einstein remind the students that in Part I of this lesson, they used word power to recognize special patterns between words. Einstein can review examples of the different word relationships with the students.

Focus/Relevancy

Einstein can tell the students that he heard some special sounds at the pond this week. He heard *plop, drop, pop,* and *clop*. Einstein can ask the students if they notice anything special about these sound words. Through discussion, elicit the idea that these words sound alike, or rhyme. Write the words on the board, and ask the students to look for a letter pattern within the words. Underline the ending letters to make the visual pattern more obvious. Ask the students what changes in each word.

OPTIONAL VARIATION: Have students use colored blocks (e.g., Lindamood blocks) to represent each sound. Point out how the colors of the blocks at the end of the words are always the same when words rhyme.

Einstein can tell the students that in today's lesson, they will have an opportunity to make their own rhyming patterns, as well as listen for these patterns in a story.

LESSON ACTIVITIES

1. Show the *Rhyming Word Patterns* poster, which lists some of the rhyming words from the story. Read the first word on the poster. Review the rhyming word pattern that focuses attention on the identical sounds of the word endings as discussed during the *focus/relevancy* section of the lesson. Let the students generate additional rhyming words that fit the pattern. Continue down the poster, letting the students give several rhyming examples for each word.

   NOTE: In the book *Each Peach Pear Plum*, not all words follow the pattern exactly (e.g., *plum/thumb*). Words that do not follow the visual rhyming pattern are not included on the poster.

2. Read the story *Each Peach Pear Plum.* Pause to let the students tell the rhyming word on each page. Emphasize the auditory pattern for the rhyming pair. In addition, students may look carefully on each page to find a particular nursery rhyme character. Discuss the different nursery rhymes and fairy tales that are included in the story.

CLOSURE

Summarize the lesson, repeat its relevance to students, and tie it to future learning. Review the rhyming word patterns that the students created, emphasizing that the ending sounds have to stay the same and that only the beginning sounds will change. Tell the students that in the next lesson, they will be using information they learned a long time ago: distinctive features.

Rhyming Word Patterns

each | **bear**
peach | **pear**

bunting | **hood**
hunting | **wood**

Jill | **ditch**
hill | **witch**

PICTURE A CLEAR DEFINITION (PART I)

GOAL

To improve expressive language skills by recognizing and generating definitions

BACKGROUND INFORMATION

The *Picture a Clear Definition* lesson is one of a series of lessons that help students develop vocabulary and higher level thinking skills, including naming antonyms, solving analogies, and defining object clearly. These lessons work to build "word power" (i.e., vocabulary knowledge and flexibility in word use).

The main emphasis of the *Picture a Clear Definition* lesson is to be aware of what makes a clear and precise definiton and to use this information when defining words. This lesson relies on the students' knowledge of a number of other lessons, especially those developing their categorization and description skills (i.e., *Alike and Different Lily Pads, Lasso the Word Herd,* and *It Makes Sense*). Students are taught that a clear definition includes a label or name, a category, a location, and a distinctive feature of the word being defined. These elements of a definition apply primarily to definitions of nouns.

OBJECTIVES

1. Identify information that makes a definition clear and precise.
2. Identify elements included in a definition pattern; namely, item name or label, category, location, and distinctive feature.
3. Generate clear, precise definitions using the definition pattern.

MATERIALS

1. Einstein character (Recommended but not necessary; see page 12.)
2. *Rhyming Directions* (See page 199.)
3. *Picture a Clear Definition* graphic (See page 200; duplicate and enlarge the graphic, color it, mount it onto colorful construction paper or poster board, and laminate it for durability, if desired.)
4. *Is Your Mamma a Llama?* (1989), by Deborah Guarino, illustrated by Steven Kellogg (This book was selected because it provides descriptions of animals that include many of the definition criteria within a fun, rhyming format. Any books that lend themselves to generating categories, locations, and features could be substituted.)
5. Pictures or objects relating to curriculum concepts in a variety of categories (e.g., fruits, animals)

INTRODUCTION

Tie-in to Prior Learning

Have Einstein remind the students that in the last lesson, they used word power to recognize special rhyming patterns between words. Using the *Rhyming Directions* from page 199, Einstein can review different rhyming patterns by having the students complete the second direction with a word that rhymes. Model a few examples before beginning (e.g., "Say *cup*. Now please stand up; Say *blow*. Now touch your toe"). Einstein can then read all but the last word of the directions and have the students guess what the rhyming word could be.

Focus/Relevancy

1. Show the *Picture a Clear Definition* poster. Ask students what they think a *definition* is. (Use a golf clap to clap out the syllables: *def/i/ni/tion.*) Refer to the poster and ask how many students have ever taken a picture. Ask what happens if the camera moves as the picture is snapped (i.e., the resulting picture will be blurry and unclear). Explain that in this lesson, the students will practice using their word power to give clear definitions of animals or objects, and that giving a clear definition is like making a sharp, clear picture in the listener's mind.

2. To illustrate the need for clear and precise definitions, intentionally model an imprecise and unclear definition while drawing parts of an animal on the board. As you draw, say:

   I'm going to give you the definition of what I'm drawing while I draw a picture on the board. See if you get a clear picture of what I'm defining.

   - *It's an animal.* (Draw an oval shape on the board.) *Do you know what animal I'm defining?* (Encourage students to generate some possibilities.) *Apparently, I'm not being clear enough! You must need more information!*
   - *It has four legs.* (Add four large legs to your drawing.) Let students generate some more possibilities. Discuss how it is often helpful when problem solving to eliminate possible alternatives. *This creature has a large body and four big legs, so we know it cannot be a snake. Name another animal that it cannot be. Do you need more information?*
   - *It's a jungle animal.* (Add a circular head to the drawing, and discuss what it could and could not be.) *I need to tell you something distinctive about this animal to make my definition clearer.*
   - *This animal has small, round ears and a large mane around his head.* (Add ears and a larger circle around the head and ears for a mane.) At this point, students should recognize the drawing as a lion. Point out that once you added the distinctive feature to the other important

information, everyone clearly knew what was being defined. *A good definition makes the meaning as clear as a photograph.*

LESSON ACTIVITIES

1. Once again, refer to the *Picture a Clear Definition* poster and emphasize the components of a good definition. Remind the students that they'll use their word power skills for naming the item, telling the category, giving a location, and telling a distinctive feature.
2. Show the cover of the book *Is Your Mamma a Llama?* Ask the students if they have ever seen a llama before. Explain that the little llama pictured on the cover uses his asking words to gather information as he searches for his mother. The animals in the story create a clear picture of their mother by including many of the parts of a good definition. Read the story and compare the definitions to the chart. Allow the students to provide missing information. Summarize each clearly before moving on (e.g., "A **bat** is an **animal** that **lives in a cave** and **comes out at night**").

   NOTE: Point out the rhyming patterns in the story to reinforce this skill.
3. To provide more opportunity for independent practice, play a game such as "I Spy." Use a group of pictures or objects relating to a variety of different categories or curriculum-related items to be defined by the students (e.g., fruits, vegetables, farm animals, or zoo animals). Students can be given a picture or object that is kept out of view to define for others using category, location, and distinctive feature. Listeners must guess the label or name of the item. Stress to the students that if their object is quickly identified, they must have been powerful speakers! Encourage the students to use the *Picture a Clear Definition* poster to help them include the important information to make their definition complete yet succinct.

   OPTIONAL VARIATION: As additional practice in a small group setting, any game board can be used. Before a student can roll the dice or spin for the number of spaces to move along the board, he or she will have to choose a picture or an object to define. (As stated above, these items may be selected at your discretion. Specific vocabulary may be chosen to suit the needs of the class theme or home environment.) The student should include all criteria for a good definition.

CLOSURE

Summarize the lesson, repeat its relevance to students, and tie it to future learning. Have the students restate the items on the *Picture a Clear Definition* poster that are necessary to tell a clear, precise definition. Stress to the students that this is a true test of their word power, since they can now give their teachers, parents, and friends picture-perfect definitions! Have Einstein tell the students that they will have an opportunity to practice giving their own definitions in the next lesson.

Rhyming Directions

Say *cup*. Now please stand (up).

Say *blow.* Now touch your (toe).

Say *treat*. Now touch your (feet).

Say *meal*. Now touch your (heel).

Say *laugh*. Now touch your (calf).

Say *tree*. Now touch your (knee).

Say *tie*. Now touch your (thigh).

Say *taste*. Now touch your (waist).

Say *yummy*. Now touch your (tummy).

Say *vest*. Now touch your (chest).

Say *boulder*. Now touch your (shoulder).

Say *charm*. Now touch your (arm).

Say *list*. Now touch your (wrist).

Say *band*. Now touch your (hand).

Say *drum*. Now touch your (thumb).

Say *peck*. Now touch your (neck).

Say *spin*. Now touch your (chin).

Say *drip*. Now touch your (lip).

Say *south*. Now touch your (mouth).

Say *chose*. Now touch your (nose).

Say *beak*. Now touch your (cheek).

Say *jack*. Now touch your (back).

Say *cry*. Now touch your (eye).

Say *dear*. Now touch your (ear).

Say *chair*. Now touch your (hair).

Say *clown*. Now please sit (down).

Picture a Clear Definition

You must tell:

1. Name: Einstein

2. Category: Frog

3. Location: He lives in a pond.

4. Feature: He learns about WORD POWER!

PICTURE A CLEAR DEFINITION (PART II)

GOAL

To improve expressive language skills by recognizing and generating definitions

BACKGROUND INFORMATION

The *Picture a Clear Definition* lesson is one of a series of lessons that help students develop vocabulary and higher level thinking skills, including naming antonyms, solving analogies, and defining objects clearly. These lessons also work to build "word power" (i.e., vocabulary knowledge and flexibility in word use).

The main emphasis of the *Picture a Clear Definition* lesson is to be aware of what makes a clear and precise definiton and to use this information when defining words. This lesson relies on the students' knowledge of a number of other lessons, especially those developing their categorization and description skills (i.e., *Alike and Different Lily Pads, Lasso the Word Herd,* and *It Makes Sense*). Students are taught that a clear definition includes a label or name, a category, a location, and a distinctive feature of the word being defined. These elements of a definition apply primarily to definitions of nouns.

In Part I, the students were introduced to the concept of a definition and a pattern for clearly communicating a definition. In Part II, the students will have the opportunity for more independent practice of this skill by playing a riddle game.

OBJECTIVES

1. Identify information that makes a definition clear and precise.
2. Identify elements included in a definition pattern: item label or name, category, location, and a distinctive feature.
3. Practice generating clear, precise definitions (riddles) using the definition pattern.

MATERIALS

1. Einstein character (Recommended but not necessary; see page 12.)
2. *Picture a Clear Definition* poster (Created earlier)
3. Simple pictures or objects of animals, household items, school items, etc. (Place in a grab bag for students to reach in and choose secretly.)

INTRODUCTION

Tie-in to Prior Learning

Have Einstein remind the students that in the last lesson, they used word power to learn about definitions. (Use a golf clap to clap out the syllables: *def/i/ni/tions.*) Ask the students what important information needs to be included. Show the *Picture a Clear Definition* poster and review. Model the use of the pattern by giving the definition of an animal from the previous lesson's story, *Is Your Mamma a Llama?* by Deborah Guarino. Examples to choose from include bat, swan, cow, kangaroo, or seal.

Focus/Relevancy

Tell the students that Einstein has a riddle for them to solve. Ask the students what a riddle is. Elicit the notion of giving important clues to lead the listener to an answer. Have Einstein say:

> *I'm thinking of something that is a kind of animal. It lives in the water and has scales and gills. What is it?* (a fish) *When I give a good definition, you should be able to picture the answer clearly in your head.*

Tell the students that they will be practicing giving their own clear definitions today.

LESSON ACTIVITIES

1. Once again, refer to the *Picture a Clear Definition* poster and emphasize the components of a good definition: naming the item, telling the category or group, giving a location, and telling a distinctive feature. Tell the students that since they are going to be asking riddles, there is one piece of the definition that they will not want to include in their riddle. Ask the students if they know which piece of information should be left out. Elicit the idea of not telling the name, although they will include all the other important facts.

2. Show the students the grab bag of objects and pictures. Tell them that they will each come up one at a time to select something from the bag. They do not want to show what the object or picture is, but they will give a riddle so that the rest of the class can guess their secret item. Use the poster to prompt the students to include the necessary information. Model the process by selecting the first item and demonstrating an appropriate riddle (e.g., "I have something that is in the cat group, lives in a jungle, and has black and orange stripes. What is it?" or "I have something that is a tool, has sharp teeth, and is used to cut wood. What is it?"). As time allows, let students practice giving and guessing the riddles.

OPTIONAL VARIATION: As additional practice in a small group setting, any game board can be used. Before a student can roll the dice or spin for the number of spaces to move along the board, he or she will have to choose a picture or an object to define. (As stated above, these items may be selected at your discretion. Specific vocabulary may be chosen to suit the needs of the class theme or home environment.) The student should include all criteria for a good definition.

CLOSURE

Summarize the lesson, repeat its relevance to students, and tie it to future learning. Have the students restate the items on the *Picture a Clear Definition* poster that are necessary to tell a clear, precise definition. Stress to the students that this is a true test of their word power, since they can now tell their teachers, parents, and friends picture-perfect definitions! Have Einstein tell the students that they have really strengthened their word power and that in the next lesson, they will have an opportunity to show off for their families again.

STRATEGY REVIEW LESSON 4

GOAL

To reinforce and review the strategies for "word power" (i.e., vocabulary knowledge and flexibility in word use) and higher level thinking skills

BACKGROUND INFORMATION

The main focus of this lesson is to review the strategies for word power and higher level thinking skills: *Learning about Opposites, Discover the Pattern*, and *Picture a Clear Definition*. A review lesson is provided after several strategies have been taught. In addition, the students take home *Homework Activity* pages and *Communication Skills Newsletter No. 4* to encourage parent involvement and understanding of the language skills.

OBJECTIVES

1. Review and practice the major components of the *Learning about Opposites, Discover the Pattern,* and *Picture a Clear Definition* strategies.
2. Complete the application activities.
3. Share strategy information with family members.

MATERIALS

1. Einstein character (Recommended but not necessary; see page 12.)
2. *Learning about Opposites* poster (Created earlier)
3. *Discover the Pattern* poster (Created earlier)
4. *Picture a Clear Definition* poster (Created earlier)
5. *Homework Activity* pages (See pages 206–207; duplicate for each student.)
6. *Skills Checklist* (See page 208; duplicate and enlarge the checklist, color it, mount it onto colorful construction paper or poster board, and laminate it, if desired.)
7. *Communication Skills Newsletter No. 4* (See pages 209–210; duplicate for each student.)

INTRODUCTION

Tie-in to Prior Learning

Einstein can remind the students that they have been learning many important skills to help them develop word power. Display and briefly review the posters and strategies for these lessons.

Focus/Relevancy

Einstein can remind the students about the last time they had homework and compliment the students on what a good job they did teaching their families about word power. He can tell them that they are going to have another special homework assignment, to be worked on with an older family member. Tell the students that their families will be really impressed when they hear how much they have learned!

LESSON ACTIVITIES

1. Briefly show the students the *Homework Activity* pages, and relate the questions on the sheets to the posters (*Learning about Opposites, Discover the Pattern, Picture a Clear Definition*) on the board.
2. Have Einstein select several students to model answers for the class, or have the entire class give choral responses to review questions from the *Homework Activity* pages.
3. Display the *Skills Checklist*. Review the key components of a lesson while looking at the poster and by practicing some items from the *Homework Activity* pages. Place or have students place a checkmark on the line beside each skill as the review is completed.
4. Show the students *Communication Skills Newsletter No. 4.* Explain that even their parents have homework. The newsletter describes the activities that they have been doing in class.
5. Hand out the *Homework Activity* pages and *Communication Skills Newsletter No. 4* for the students to take home, or place them in envelopes for students to take home.

CLOSURE

Summarize the lesson, repeat its relevance to students, and tie it to future learning. Have Einstein encourage the students to share their *Homework Activities* pages and *Communication Skills Newsletter No. 4* with someone special at home. Explain that after they have completed the homework, they should have their parent or caregiver sign and date in the appropriate space and return it for a reward (e.g., a sticker or points on a homework chart). Have Einstein tell the students that in the next lesson, they will be starting a brand-new unit, which will require them to use their best listening skills and word power.

Homework Activity

Name: ____________________

Discover the pattern. Make the connection. Solve the puzzle!

o : O :: ❑ : ?

1. **Wheel goes with car the way**

   leaf goes with ________________.

2. **Lemon goes with sour the way**

   sugar goes with ________________.

Antonyms
tell the opposite!

NOT COLD BUT HOT

...not big but

____

...not fast but

____

...not long but

____

Family Member: ________________ Date: ________________

Homework Activity

Name: ____________________

Discover the rhyming pattern! How many rhymes can you think of?

coat	reach	bat
goat	peach	cat
________	________	________

Tell the important information to

Picture a Clear Definition

Tell the...

1. Name: "It's called a ____________."
2. Category or group: "It's a kind of ____________."
3. Location: "You find it ____________."
4. Feature (something special about it): "____________."

Give a clear definition for each of the following:

1. lion
2. snow
3. pencil
4. scissors
5. daisy
6. banana

Family Member: ____________________ Date: ____________

Skills Checklist

Skill ✓ Up

I've been learning about WORD POWER!

1. I can "say it another way."
big or large; little or small ______

2. Opposites are completely different.
I can tell opposites!
up/down, in/out, stop/go ______

3. Analogies: These are fun! I can solve word puzzles by discovering the pattern! *"Cow* goes with *moo* the way *chicken* goes with *cluck!"* ______

4. Patterns are all around! I can *listen* for and *look* for *rhyming* patterns: c*at,* h*at*, m*at*. ______

5. I can give a def/i/ni/tion by telling the most important information: "A *lion* is a *jungle animal* that has a *mane* (or roars)." ______

The next unit will be all about a story recipe.
I will create my own stories!

COMMUNICATION SKILLS NEWSLETTER

No. 4

MORE WORD POWER!!

Your child has continued to develop "word power"! Since becoming experts at categorizing and comparing and contrasting, we learned several ways to build vocabulary and use words in different ways. You'll read about those different ways in this newsletter!

The Power of Opposites

We learned that some words are antonyms, or *opposites*. It helps to think of opposites by putting words into a phrase, "It's not hot, it's ____." We read the story, *That's Good! That's Bad!* by Margery Cuyler. This story provided many words to practice our sentence strategy, such as, "It's not ***high***, it's ***low***." (Others include: shiny/dull, little/big, tall/short, clean/dirty, noisy/quiet, play/work, lost/found, back/front, up/down, stop/go, asleep/awake, mom/dad, day/night, dark/light). The students needed their active listening skills to catch the occasional "slip" of an incorrect opposite word within the story. You might want to keep your child on his or her toes when listening to a story by including an occasional "mistake" when you read. Have your child tell the opposite word that fits so that the story makes sense.

It's not high, it's low.

It's not ______________, it's ______________.

The Power of Rhyming Words

After practicing with word associations and various patterns, we thought more about patterns by listening for rhyming words. This skill requires an awareness of sounds and the ability to recognize similar ending sounds auditorally (hearing) and visually (seeing written patterns). We read the story *Each Peach Pear Plum,* by Janet and Allan Ahlberg. The students predicted rhyming words within the story. We also looked at some words within the story to see the pattern (e.g., *pear/bear*). Notice the rhyming words in the stories, or fun rhymes and riddles that you share with your child. See how many different words your child can think of that fit a rhyming pattern.

pear/bear

fun/sun

cake/take

rug/tug

The Power of Association Patterns

We talked about patterns, and your child helped predict what would come next in a pattern. Talk about the patterns below and have your child describe what would come next.

Your child also practiced recognizing common association patterns, such as **categories** (*cat* goes with *pets*), **antonyms** (*up* goes with *down*), **function** (*pencil* goes with *write*), **feature** (*apple* goes with *red*), **part-whole** (*wheel* goes with *bicycle*), and **location** (*cow* goes with *barn*). This is definitely a higher level thinking skill and one that students will use in many school tasks. They did an excellent job!

Looking Ahead to What Is Next!

I hope that you will use this information and these ideas to continue to practice these skills at home with your child. In our last unit, we will be moving on to develop our story knowledge. We'll talk about the parts of a good story and much more. Now would be a good time to make a trip to the library and check out some fun storybooks.

The Power of Definitions

We studied the important information that needs to be included when telling what a word means. We compared a good definition to a photograph, because it helps the listener "picture" the word meaning as clearly as looking at a picture.

We read the book *Is Your Mamma a Llama?* by Deborah Guarino, and practiced using the fun, rhyming information to tell clear definitions. We used a pattern to give a complete definition, which included the **name**, the **group** ("It's a kind of ____."), the **location** or place where it can be found, and a **feature** that makes it special or different from others within that group. The story gave some of the information we needed for our definition (e.g., "she hangs by her feet and lives in a cave"), so we knew that a **bat** is a kind of **animal**, that **lives in a cave** and **likes to hang upside down,** or that **comes out at night**, etc.

Play "I'm Thinking of Something" with your child. Give the *important definition clues,* and have your child complete it by telling the name (e.g., "I'm thinking of something that is a kind of *tool*. It's found in the garage or in a toolbox, and it's used to tighten screws. What is it?"). Take turns giving riddles and compliment your child on giving the most important information.

UNIT THREE

STORY RECIPE: STORY KNOWLEDGE (PART I)

GOAL

To improve story knowledge

BACKGROUND INFORMATION

The main focus of the *Story Recipe* lesson is to improve students' overall narrative language skills by introducing the essential story grammar components and by helping students use these components to create their own stories. Before students can be expected to tell, retell, and eventually write clear and logical stories, they must first be able to identify story grammar elements. These are the elements that help a story flow. They will be referred to as *story ingredients* in this lesson. Many variations of story grammar elements exist; the elements used in the *Story Recipe* strategy include setting (time, place, and characters), problem, solution, and outcome.

OBJECTIVES

1. Identify story grammar components in a story (i.e., setting [time, place, and characters], problem, solution, and outcome).
2. Identify story grammar components in a reading activity.

MATERIALS

1. Einstein character (Recommended but not necessary; see page 12.)
2. Social application story: *Einstein Shares His Story Knowledge* (See pages 215–220; also see page 7.)
3. Any book that includes a setting, problem, solution, and outcome (e.g., *Possum Magic,* 1991, by Mem Fox, illustrated by Julie Vivas; *The Princess and the Pea,* 1979, by Hans Christian Andersen, illustrated by Paul Galdone; *Mufaro's Beautiful Daughters,* 1987, by John Steptoe, translated by Clarita Kohen). Most fairy tales will also work.

   NOTE: If a favorite story does not expressly state one of the story ingredients, this should be added as the story is read. Except for *The Princess and the Pea,* the books listed include all the "story recipe" ingredients. When a story ingredient is not mentioned, you will need to provide the missing ingredient (e.g., since the setting is not directly stated in this story, the illustration can be used to discuss a setting or the educator can begin the story with "Long ago in a castle...").

4. *Story Recipe* graphic (See page 221; duplicate and enlarge the graphic, color it, mount it onto colorful construction paper or poster board, and laminate it for durability, if desired.)

5. A large, clear mixing bowl filled with warm water, yellow and red food coloring, gold glitter, a small amount of dry ice (hidden from view in a container with an airtight lid), a spoon, and a scoop or tongs for handling the dry ice

INTRODUCTION

Tie-in to Prior Learning

Have Einstein remind the students that in the last lesson, they used word power to make definitions. He can emphasize that when they tell the category, location, and distinctive feature of an object, the listener will be able to picture the object clearly and to tell what it is.

Focus/Relevancy

Einstein can tell the students that he would like to tell them about an interesting experience that he had over the weekend. Read and discuss the social application story *Einstein Shares His Story Knowledge.*

LESSON ACTIVITIES

1. Discuss the meaning of the word *ingredients,* and ask what the students think of when they hear that word. Compare telling or writing a story to following a recipe. Ask the students what would happen if someone left out the sugar when baking a cake or cookies. Show the *Story Recipe* poster, and explain that a story has key ingredients just like a recipe and that if you leave out one of the story ingredients, your story won't be complete. If you include all the ingredients, then you have the first step in developing story knowledge. Highlight and discuss each story ingredient listed on the poster.

2. Explain to the students that as you read the story, they are to give the thumbs-up signal whenever they hear one of the story ingredients. Read the story and compliment their CAREful listening. As you read, point out the following literary highlights:

   - Story knowledge elements. As the story ingredients are mentioned and the students signal, stop and ask which part of the recipe they heard.

   - Read through the problem as mentioned in the story. Stop and ask if this is a good place for the story to end. Do we know what happens to the characters? Ask if there are any unanswered questions.

3. After you read the story, act out "mixing" a story by following the story recipe as follows:

   "You have the ingredients for making a good story, so let's 'mix' a story as we review our new story knowledge." As you are saying this, place the bowl of water where the students can see it.

   Ask the students what the first story ingredient is. Elicit *setting* and discuss how the setting is made of time (when), place (where), and characters (who) as related to the story. (Point this out on the poster.) Say, "The setting—when, where, and who—will be the first ingredient in our special recipe." (Add a pinch of gold glitter for each part of the setting [3 pinches] to the water and stir.) Allow the students to comment on what they observe.

   Ask if the story is complete. Ask, "What story ingredient is needed next?" Encourage the students to use the graphic as a reference to elicit *problem* as the next ingredient. (Add several drops of yellow food coloring and stir.) Allow brief comments on observed changes.

   Ask what the next story ingredient will be. Relate to the *solution* from the previously read story. (Add several drops of red food coloring and mix together.) Let the students make observations about the changes to their mixture.

   Ask what the last story ingredient is. Elicit *outcome*. Tell the students that when we include the outcome, we will have created a good story. Continue by explaining that there is another secret ingredient that will add "spice" to our story to make it even better. Tell the students that this secret ingredient is often used to create an outcome that is unexpected or a surprise. The secret ingredient is *imagination*. (At the same time, carefully add a small chunk of dry ice to the bowl.) The students are usually surprised when you add *imagination* to *outcome*.

CLOSURE

Summarize the lesson, repeat its relevance to students, and tie it to future learning. Einstein can congratulate the students on their new story knowledge. He can ask the students to look at the poster and "read" the ingredients that a story needs. Relate the use of imagination to the story that was read in class. Tell the students that in the next lesson, they will be using the story recipe and their imagination to create a special class story.

One day, Einstein was skipping home from school with a note that a storyteller was coming to visit his class. Suddenly, the note slipped from his hand and floated into the tall grass beside the pond.

1

When he went to get it, he heard, "I don't know why you're so excited. A silly old storyteller sounds boring to me. What's so special about listening to stories anyway?" asked Buddy Worm.

2

"Well," Einstein began, "have you ever sailed in a great ship across an ocean or traveled to India to ride on an elephant's back?"

"No!" Buddy Worm replied. "Have you?" he asked.

"Yes. When I use my imagination, stories take me on adventures!"

3

"I like to listen to the story and try to guess or predict what will happen next…and sometimes I am very surprised!" Einstein exclaimed. "One story had a pirate who found a buried treasure. When he opened the lid and looked inside, his mouth fell open. What do you think was inside?"

"I don't know," responded Buddy.

"Guess," challenged Einstein. "When we use our story knowledge to predict, we can guess anything…gold, jewels, or even pickles!"

The worm laughed. "Okay, I guess that it was full of…apples! That would be a treasure for a worm!"

"Great! When you make predictions, you're using story knowledge to become a better thinker!" explained Einstein.

Einstein told Buddy Worm that one day his mom asked why there was a fire truck outside their school. "I used my story knowledge to tell about the firefighter who visited with our class and shared the equipment on his fire truck," explained Einstein.

6

"If I had story knowledge, I might tell about things I see and do!" thought Buddy.

7

That very evening, Einstein, Buddy Worm, and their scout troop went on a campout. As the dinner activities quieted and the sun went down, Einstein and Buddy Worm began to hear grumbles from the other campers. "What will we do now? There are no TVs, video games, or computers. We're bored!"

As they sat around the campfire, Buddy and Einstein smiled at each other and said, "Stories are fun! What we need is a good storyteller!"

8

Each scout took a turn telling a story that evening. Buddy and Einstein told the best stories. They all agreed that telling stories was a lot of fun.

9

With story knowledge, we can *tell about* the things we *see and do!*

With story knowledge, we can *HAVE FUN!*

10

With story knowledge, we can use our *imaginations* and go on *adventures!*

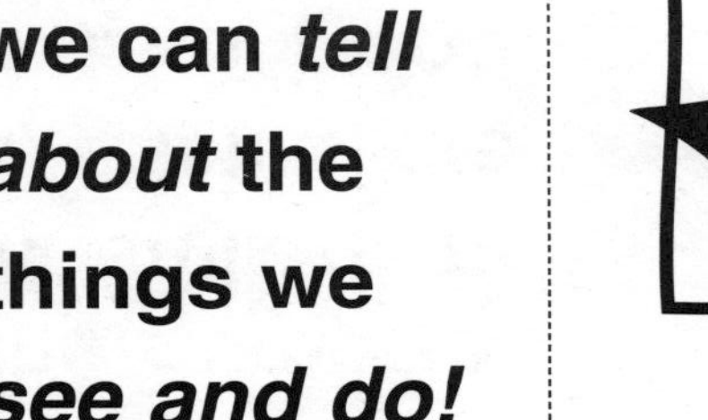

With story knowledge, we can make *predictions* and become *good thinkers!*

11

Know The... Story Recipe

I. setting

A. when

B. where

C. who

II. problem

III. solution

IV. outcome

STORY RECIPE: STORY KNOWLEDGE (PART II)

GOAL

To improve story knowledge

BACKGROUND INFORMATION

The main focus of the *Story Recipe* lesson is to improve students' overall narrative language skills by introducing the essential story grammar components and helping students use these components to create their own stories. Before students can be expected to tell, retell, and eventually write clear and logical stories, they must first be able to identify story grammar elements. These are the elements that help a story flow. They are referred to as *story ingredients* in this lesson. Many variations of story grammar elements exist; the elements used in the *Story Recipe* strategy include setting (time, place, and characters), problem, solution, and outcome.

OBJECTIVES

1. Identify story grammar components in a story (i.e., setting [time, place, and characters], problem, solution, and outcome).
2. Use story grammar components to create a story by selecting an example of each ingredient when given several choices.

MATERIALS

1. Einstein character (Recommended but not necessary; see page 12.)
2. Social application story: *Einstein Shares His Story Knowledge* (Created earlier)
3. *Story Recipe* poster (Created earlier)
4. Chalkboard and chalk
5. *Story Strips* (See pages 224–225; duplicate them, cut them out, and laminate them for durability, if desired. Use tape or magnets to place them on the board.)

INTRODUCTION

Tie-in to Prior Learning

Have Einstein remind the students that in the last lesson, they "mixed" something very special. Discuss what the class created with their special ingredients. Let students name the ingredients that every good story should have.

Focus/Relevancy

Show the picture of the worm from the social application story. Ask the students if they remember what Einstein was trying to teach Buddy, who wasn't very interested in stories. Elicit the benefits of having story knowledge by showing the checklist from the story. Explain to the students that now that they know the ingredients, they can use their story knowledge to create a good story.

LESSON ACTIVITIES

1. Show the *Story Recipe* poster, and have the students "read" the ingredients aloud as you write the words across the top of the board. Tell the students that you are going to read some examples of story ingredients and that their job will be to decide which kind of ingredient is written on the strip (e.g., show a *Story Strip* that says "Long, long ago" or "deep in the forest"). The students will decide where to place it on the board. Elicit the concepts of when and where as being part of the setting, and place the strip under the word *setting*). After all the *Story Strips* have been read and placed on the board, go back and read each group again.
2. Tell the students that even though they now have the ingredients to create a new story, there is a problem. Explain that since there are too many examples for each ingredient, they will have to vote for one item in each group. Ask if they have ever voted in their classroom before. Tell the students that they will vote by using a "show of hands." This means that the teacher will count the number of hands raised for each choice. The winning choice will be the one that has the most votes, or the biggest number of hands raised. Remind the students that they can vote only one time for each ingredient, unless more than one of an ingredient is called for. After reading the choices under each ingredient and letting the students vote, leave only the "winners" on the board. After the voting is complete, have the students chorally read their new story.

CLOSURE

Summarize the lesson, repeat its relevance to students, and tie it to future learning. Have Einstein compliment the students on the story they created using the story recipe by telling a setting, problem, solution, and outcome. Explain that in the next lesson, they will get more practice in using their story knowledge skills by telling the parts of a story in a certain order. With story knowledge, they can become expert storytellers!

Story Strips

NOTE: Add some small connecting words for the story to flow as the strips are read.

Setting ***(When)***

Long, long, ago

Last Saturday

One dark, stormy night

(Where)

in a castle

deep in the forest

on a deserted island

(Who) **(Choose two innocent people and one villain.)**

the beautiful princess

the handsome prince

the kind king

the evil queen

the wicked wizard

Problem

(Villain) **cast a spell that made** (innocent person) **and** (innocent person) **turn into armadillos.**

(Villain) **cast a spell that made** (innocent person) **and** (innocent person) **turn into big green toads.**

(Villain) **cast a spell that made** (innocent person) **and** (innocent person) **turn purple.**

(Villain) **cast a spell that made** (innocent person) **and** (innocent person) **fall asleep.**

Solution

When (villain) **was captured, the spell was broken.**

They hired a superhero, who broke the spell and changed them back to normal.

Mrs. (a familiar teacher's name) **discovered the secret and broke the spell.**

Outcome

They lived happily ever after.

They moved to (location) **and opened a restaurant.**

They never saw (villain) **again.**

FOLLOW THE DETAIL TRAIL: SEQUENCING (PART I)

GOAL

To improve story knowledge

BACKGROUND INFORMATION

The main focus of the *Follow the Detail Trail: Sequencing* lesson is to improve the students' overall story knowledge by using sequencing words, such as *first, next, then,* and *finally*, to put events in order. The students develop the understanding that stories have a beginning, a middle, and an end. In Part I of this lesson, students use sequence words to put stories in order.

OBJECTIVES

1. Identify the sequence of events from a story.
2. Use sequence words to place events in order to retell a story.

MATERIALS

1. Einstein character (Recommended but not necessary; see page 12.)
2. *Follow the Detail Trail* graphic (See page 229; duplicate and enlarge the graphic, color it, mount it onto colorful construction paper or poster board, and laminate it for durability, if desired.)
3. *"Einstein's Day" Sentence Strips* (See page 230; duplicate and enlarge the strips, cut them apart, and laminate them for durability, if desired. Use tape or magnets to place them on the board.)
4. *The Mitten* (1989), by Jan Brett (This book was chosen because of the beautiful illustrations; the clues for predicting, which are included on each page; the vocabulary; and the fun story. The educator could choose any story that has easily recognized events that can be sequenced.)
5. *Mitten Sentences* (See page 231–232; duplicate and enlarge the mittens, color them, cut them apart, and laminate them for durability, if desired. Use tape or magnets to place them on the board.)

INTRODUCTION

Tie-in to Prior Learning

Einstein can remind the students of the story that they created in the last lesson by voting for their favorite ingredient choices. Ask the students how the story could have been changed by using a different setting, characters, problem, solution, or outcome. Tell the students they can retell this story or make up a new story by including all the ingredients.

Focus/Relevancy

Einstein can tell the students that he recently called Grandma Froggie to tell her about his day. He told her that he caught a fly for lunch, learned a new dive after school, ate mosquito pancakes for breakfast, and learned to group beetles by size and color in math class. His poor granny was so confused! She told Einstein to put his day in order. Show the *Follow the Detail Trail* poster, and note the sequencing, or order, words that are listed. Tell the students that Einstein can tell about his day by using the words *first, next, then,* and *finally*.

LESSON ACTIVITIES

1. Show the students the *"Einstein's Day" Sentence Strips.* Let the students help Einstein organize his ideas by reviewing events cited above (see *focus/relevancy*) using sequence, or order, words (e.g., *First,* Einstein ate mosquito pancakes. *Next,* he sorted beetles in math. *Then...*). Emphasize the sequence words as the children use them in their answers while placing the corresponding strip on the board. Let the students chorally "read" or tell about Einstein's day, using sequence words and the sentence strips on the board. (You may want to write the appropriate sequence word in front of each sentence strip on the board.)

2. Present the book *The Mitten* to the students. While showing the cover of the book, discuss the title and the author. Let the students predict what the story might be about. Let the students show how it would feel if they lived in the climate that is depicted on the book's cover (e.g., the students could show that they were cold by doing a shivering motion). Tell the students that the story is based on a Ukrainian folktale. Compare and contrast what they notice about the weather, clothing, and housing from the pictured culture with that of their own community.

3. Tell the students that their job for this lesson will be to listen to and remember when the different events in the story occur. They will see some of these events again. Read the story *The Mitten.* Talk about the author's use of picture clues on the side of each page, which help the students predict what might happen next in the story. Point out the following literary highlights:

   Vocabulary: *Baba, tunneling, burrow, snuffling, jostled, prickles, commotion, swooped, glinty, talons, snug, waft, investigate, drowsy, muzzle, lumbered, bulged, silhouetted*

   Figurative language: *white as snow, safe and sound, big kickers, diggers, held fast*

4. Review the sequence words that help us put events in order (e.g., *first, next, then, finally*). Display the *Mitten Sentences* out of sequence and read them. Let the students tell which event shows how the story began, and place it on the left side of the board. Find the sentences that tell what

happened in the middle of the story, and place them using *next* and *then*, in order on the board, and use *finally* to show how the story ended. Then read the mittens from left to right across the board.

HINT

For an added effect, draw a line to represent a clothesline on the board so that the mittens may be "hung up" in order.

CLOSURE

Summarize the lesson, repeat its relevance to students, and tie it to future learning. Stress that stories can be very confusing if they are told out of order or without words that signal when each event happened. Compliment the students on their ability to listen to a story and use their order words to retell the events of the story. Explain that telling their ideas in order is an important skill to practice, and that in the next lesson, Einstein will have a tricky activity that depends on telling the steps to do a job in order.

FOLLOW THE DETAIL TRAIL
FIRST
NEXT
FINALLY
THEN

"Einstein's Day" Sentence Strips

caught a fly for lunch

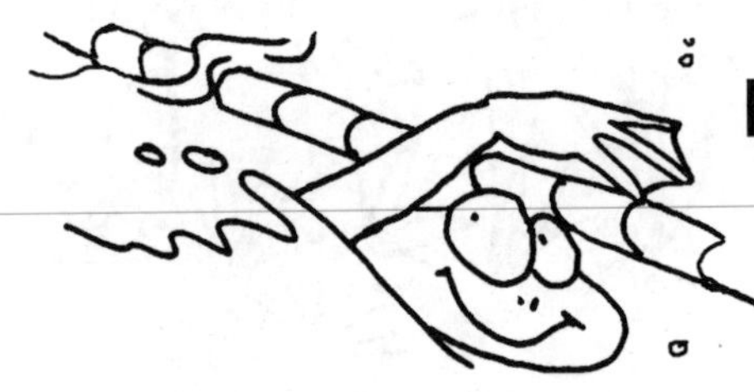

learned a new dive after school

ate mosquito pancakes for breakfast

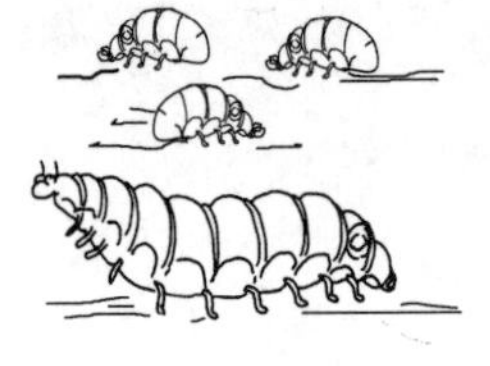
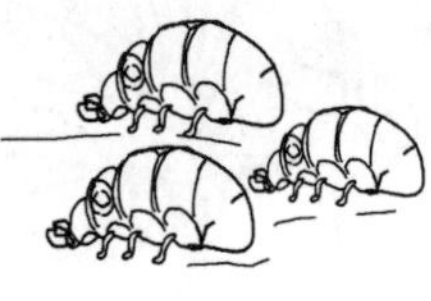

learned to group beetles by size and color in math

Mitten Sentences

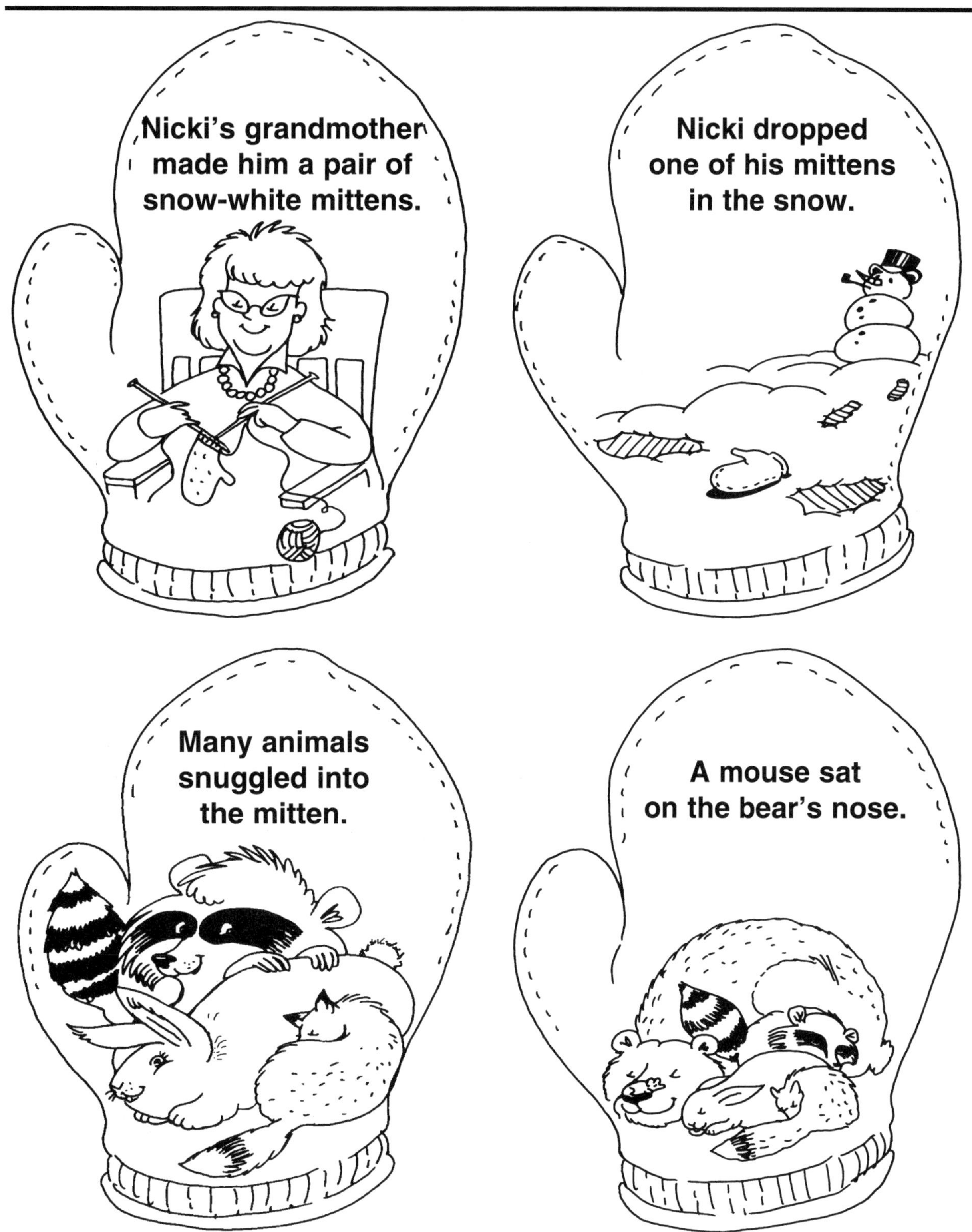

The bear gave an enormous sneeze that scattered all the animals into the snow.
Nicki found his lost mitten.

FOLLOW THE DETAIL TRAIL: SEQUENCING (PART II)

GOAL

To improve story knowledge

BACKGROUND INFORMATION

The main focus of the *Follow the Detail Trail: Sequencing* lesson is to improve the students' overall story knowledge by using sequencing words, such as *first, next, then,* and *finally,* to put events in order. The students develop the understanding that stories have a beginning, a middle, and an end. In Part II of this lesson, students use sequence words to order the steps for a task.

OBJECTIVES

1. Identify the sequence of events to complete a task.
2. Use sequence words to explain the steps for completing a task.

MATERIALS

1. Einstein character (Recommended but not necessary; see page 12.)
2. Notecards (3 x 5") with the words *first, next, then,* and *finally* written on them (Laminate for durability, if desired.)
3. Newspaper pages or paper approximately the size of a newspaper page (One per student for making paper hats)
4. *Hat Sequence* (See page 237.)
5. *Follow the Detail Trail* poster (Created earlier)

INTRODUCTION

Tie-in to Prior Learning

Have Einstein remind the students that they helped him learn to use special words to tell about the events of his day so that Granny Frog would not be confused. Let the students tell the words that help organize our ideas, whether telling about our day or the events in a story. Review *first, next, then,* and *finally* by posting the cards with these words written on them.

Focus/Relevancy

Tell the students about a day at the pond when a rabbit was explaining to Einstein that he had learned a way to help the environment by planting an oak tree where other trees had been chopped down. He asked Einstein for some help since he didn't know all the important steps for this job. Ask the students,

"What do you think Einstein told him to do?" Elicit student responses. Say, "Rabbit asked, 'Does it matter what order you do the steps in?' What do you think Einstein said?" Elicit student responses.

Tell the students that they will continue to use those important sequence, or order, words when they tell how to do something.

LESSON ACTIVITIES

1. Explain that students will practice using their sequence words to tell how to complete a job. Choose four students to line up in front of the class shoulder to shoulder. Give each an index card in a left to right sequence: *first, next, then,* and *finally*. Explain that they will work as a team, telling the class how to make something or do a job. They are each to give a step starting with the special sequence word that is written on their card. Each group will sequence one task. Tell the students to act out the instruction given as they listen to the steps (e.g., if a student says to stir the ingredients, model that for the students and have them all participate by pantomiming the stirring step). If necessary, prompt the students to give the most important steps and to provide an ending step. The following are suggested tasks to sequence, but you may choose others. All students should have an opportunity to participate in a group of four before moving on to Activity 2.

   Suggested Tasks to Sequence

   - Making a peanut butter sandwich
   - Making lemonade or juice
   - Checking out a book
   - Making a sandcastle
   - Making popcorn
   - Brushing teeth
   - Getting ready for school
   - Getting ready for a picnic
   - Planting a seed

2. Explain to the students that in the next activity, they will be listening for the important steps to make something tricky and that Einstein will give them the important steps.

HINT

It helps to keep children on task by making this an "Einstein Says" (similar to "Simon Says") activity.

Pass a large, newspaper-sized piece of paper to each student. (This should be one full sheet folded vertically along the center so that it forms a 22 x 13 ½" rectangle. This gives the hat some weight. If the educator is using thicker paper, simply measure it to be approximately 22 x 13 ½".) Explain that they will need to listen for what to do *first, next, then,* and *finally* so that they will have something special to wear when they are finished. Do not tell them what they are making. Give the following directions (see page 237 for a pictorial representation of these directions) while modeling each step:

a. *Einstein says you should* first *lay your paper so that it goes up and down like so* (demonstrate laying the paper so that it makes a vertical rectangle).

b. *Einstein says* next *you should next make a 'taco fold' by matching the corners so that your taco opening is closest to your tummy* (demonstrate).

c. *Einstein says* then *you should pinch the middle of the page at the top with your left hand and fold the right corner down to make a straight line going down from the pinched spot. It makes a triangle shape and leaves a paper flap below the triangle. Press along the fold to crease the paper* (demonstrate).

d. *Einstein says* next *you should put one hand on the triangle-shaped flap and fold the left corner down to make a matching triangle on the left side. Press along the fold to crease the paper* (demonstrate).

HINT

You may want to have some tape available so that, as the students finish this step and quietly raise their hand to show that they are ready, each student can be given a piece of tape that is long enough to go across the two triangle flaps. This will make the next step easier. Tell the students to offer help if their neighbor is having trouble folding.

Use the "Einstein Says" activity to help keep the students quiet and attending by saying, for example, "Did Einstein say 'Talk to your neighbor' or 'Play with your paper'? Remember to do what Einstein says!"

e. *Einstein says* finally *you should fold the flap at the bottom up, turn the whole paper over, and fold the flap on the other side up as well* (demonstrate). *Now, open the bottom and put on your…hat!*

CLOSURE

Summarize the lesson, repeat its relevance to students, and tie it to future learning. Stress that activities can be very confusing if they are told out of order or without words that signal when each step should happen. Review the *Follow the Detail Trail: Sequencing* poster. Compliment the students on their ability to listen to and use their sequence, or order, words to tell how to do different things. Tell the students that since they have become experts at telling what happens *first, next, then,* and *finally* in a story or job, in the next lesson, they will be practicing their story knowledge in a new and different way!

Hat Sequence

1.

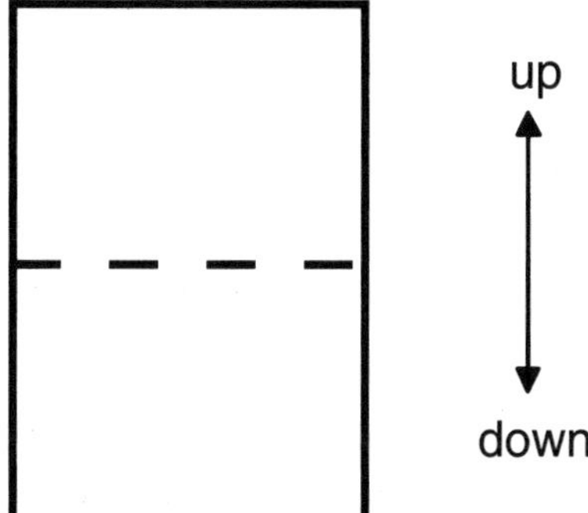

2.

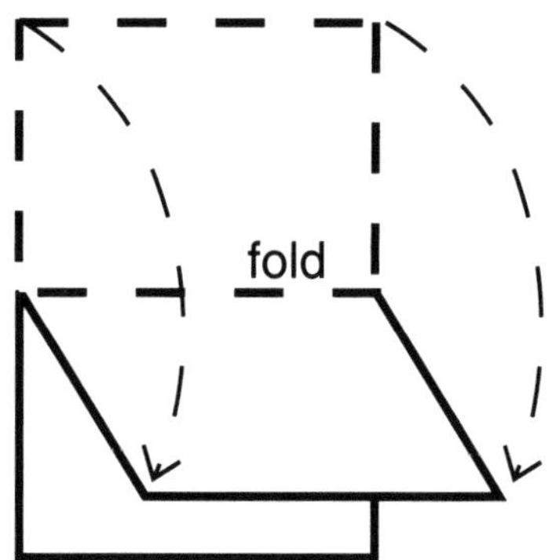

3.

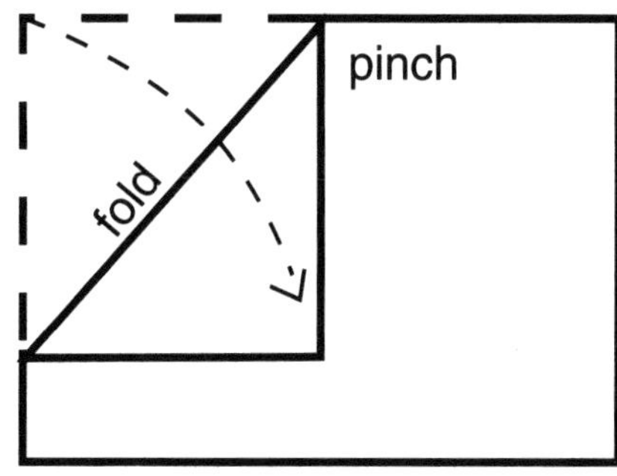

then

4.

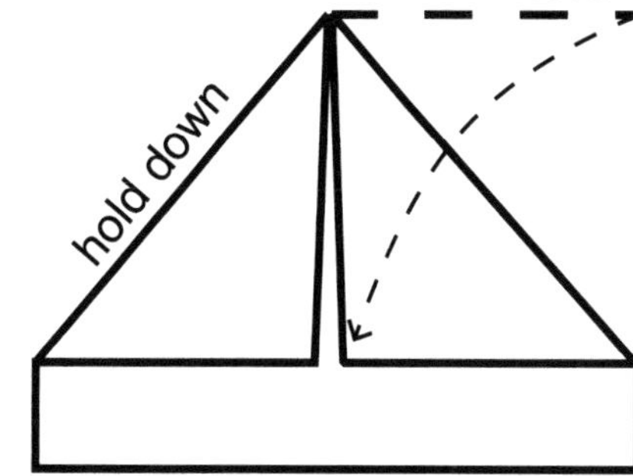

5.

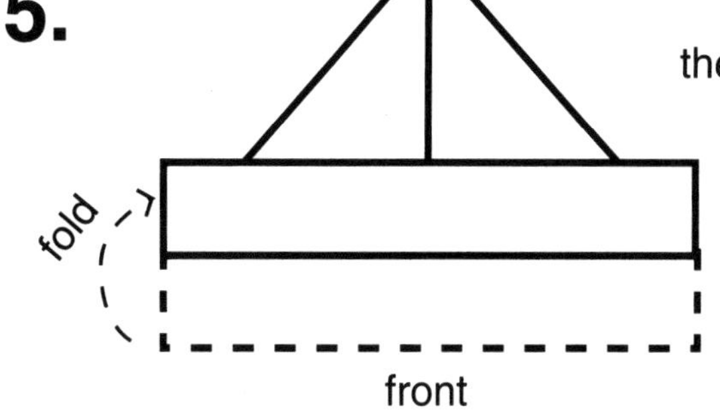

then turn over

TELL THE BIGGEST EGGS: MAIN IDEA

GOAL

To improve story knowledge

BACKGROUND INFORMATION

The main focus of this lesson is to improve the students' overall story knowledge by helping them learn to summarize a story. Students learn to tell what a story is mainly about by following a pattern that highlights telling the main character(s) and the most important problem or event in one or two sentences. This strategy is referred to as *Tell the Biggest Eggs!*

Note: Before students can be expected to tell the main idea of a story, they will need to be able to identify the story grammar elements (see the *Story Recipe* lesson).

OBJECTIVE

1. Tell what a story is mainly about by following a pattern that highlights the main character(s) and primary problem or event as the "main idea."

MATERIALS

1. Einstein character (Recommended but not necessary; see page 12.)
2. *Follow the Detail Trail* poster (Created earlier)
3. Seven plastic eggs (Two large and five small eggs; prepared as in Activity 1)
4. *Story Detail Strips* (See page 242; prepared as in Activity 1.)
5. Wire or straw basket to hold the eggs
6. *Alexander and the Terrible, Horrible, No Good, Very Bad Day* (1972), by Judith Viorst, illustrated by Ray Cruz (This book was chosen because of the easily recognizable main character and primary problem. Any story lending itself to easy identification of these story grammar elements could be used.)
7. Chalkboard and chalk
8. *Tell the Biggest Eggs* graphic (See page 243; duplicate and enlarge the graphic, color it, mount it onto colorful construction paper or poster board, and laminate it for durability, if desired.)

INTRODUCTION

Tie-in to Prior Learning

Have Einstein ask the students what they learned in the last lessons that helped them tell stories or how to complete a job. Show the *Follow the Detail Trail: Sequencing* poster, and briefly review the sequence words.

Focus/Relevancy

Tell the students that Einstein went to visit his cousin at a pond near a farm. He saw all kinds of animals that don't live near his pond. Have the students find the person to their right and whisper the name of a farm animal. Have the students raise their hand if they heard: *cow, pig, horse, dog, cat, chicken, sheep, duck, goose* (allow time after each animal name for the students to raise their hand). Tell the students that as Einstein watched the noisy chickens clucking about the coop, he noticed something unusual about their eggs. Show the basket of eggs, and ask the students what they notice about the eggs. (If prepared as described in Activity 1 of this lesson, there should be two eggs that are larger than the others.) Ask the students to "decide and hide" (show with their fingers the number of large eggs, but hide that number of fingers in their other hand) how many of the eggs are larger. When you ask for the answer, they may all show their number by holding up their fingers. They should all have seen two large eggs.

Explain that these two eggs are very important for today's story knowledge lesson. In this lesson, they will learn that sometimes it is important to be able to tell what a story is mostly about, without telling the whole story. Explain that the two large eggs will help them to tell what the story is mostly about without "clucking out the whole story" and that they will soon know the secret of the large eggs.

LESSON ACTIVITIES

1. Before this lesson, create a set of eggs as follows: label the two large eggs as "Main Character(s)" and "Main Problem or Event"; label each of the small eggs "Details." Enlarge and duplicate one set of *Story Detail Strips* onto heavy stock paper, and cut them apart to form strips. Duplicate and decrease in size another set of *Story Detail Strips*. Cut the strips apart and place them in the eggs, sorting according to "main" information (large eggs) or details (small eggs).

2. Temporarily set the basket of eggs aside and introduce the book *Alexander and the Terrible, Horrible, No Good, Very Bad Day*, by Judith Viorst. Ask the students what they notice about the boy pictured on the cover and what they think the story is mostly about. Call on one or two students to share their predictions, with the others in the class showing agreement with their golf clap. Read the story. Encourage the group to "read along" each time the story comes to "I could tell it was going to be...(pause for students to join in)...a terrible, horrible, no good, very bad day!"

   As you are reading the story, point out the following literary highlights:

   Vocabulary: *skateboard, breakfast, mistake, code ring, secret agent, Australia, car pool, carsick, invisible, tack, dentist, cavity, scolded*

3. Once again, show the basket of eggs. Have students come up one at a time to open the eggs, beginning with the small eggs. Read the *Story Detail Strip* inside, and tape the larger corresponding *Story Detail Strip* on a wall or bulletin board for easier reading. After reading the strip on the board, ask the students if it tells who or what the story is mostly about (e.g., "Is this story mostly about having bubble gum in your hair, or is that just one of the details?"). Explain that details give more information about the characters and problems or events. To illustrate a main idea, save the largest eggs for the end. Again highlight the labels on the outside that say "Main Character(s)" and "Main Problem or Event." Read and tape the large, corresponding strips to the board. Ask, "Is this story mostly about a boy named Alexander? Is this story mostly about Alexander having a bad day?" Upon reading these strips, you may wish to hang them away from the others to illustrate the concept of telling these two ingredients for the main idea.

4. To practice the *Tell the Biggest Eggs* strategy, tell the students that you will call them up in pairs to summarize a story by telling the main character(s) and the main problem or event. Write "________ is mostly about ________ who ________." Read the sentence and give them an example ("*Alexander and the Terrible, Horrible, No Good, Very Bad Day* is mostly about a boy named Alexander who has a terrible day"). Tell the students that as each pair comes up, the whole class will need to help by asking a very important question. Write "What is it about?" on the board. Practice reading the question chorally. To give an example, tell the students, "I read *The Paper Bag Princess,* by Robert N. Munsch." Prompt the class to respond by pointing to the question on the board, "What is it about?" Point to the pattern on the board and read aloud, "***The Paper Bag Princess*** is mostly about **a princess** who **saves a prince from the dragon that burned up her castle.**" Tell them that sometimes when you try to tell the biggest eggs it is very hard not to "cluck out the whole story"! Using the list below, or familiar stories used in the classroom, tell each pair the name of the story they are to summarize as they come up. Have them say, "We know a story called ________." Prompt the class to respond by reading their question. Choose one student to tell the main character(s) and the other to tell the main problem or event. Continue for each pair, prompting with the patterns as necessary.

Story Summary List

The Three Bears

Cinderella

The Three Pigs

101 Dalmatians

The Princess and the Pea

The Little Mermaid

Little Red Riding Hood

Dumbo

That's Good! That's Bad!

The Three Little Javalinas

The Very Quiet Cricket

Too Much Noise

The Very Hungry Caterpillar

The Mitten

CLOSURE

Summarize the lesson, repeat its relevance to students, and tie it to future learning. Remind the students that sometimes they will need to tell the most important parts of the story, rather than telling a detail or "clucking out the whole story"! Present the *Tell the Biggest Eggs* poster. Have the students tell Einstein what the "biggest eggs" should tell about the story (i.e., main character[s] and main problem or event). Explain that in the next lesson, Einstein will be a detective and will be following the *Detail Trail* of a story.

Story Detail Strips

Main Character

Alexander

Main Problem or Event

He had a terrible, horrible, no good, very bad day.

Details

He got soap in his eye.

He didn't get any dessert.

He got a cavity.

He got gum in his hair.

Characters

Mom

Dad

brothers

teacher

Main Idea...
"Tell The BIGGEST Eggs"
SETTING (where)
OUTCOME
DETAILS
SETTING (when)
SOLUTION
MAIN CHARACTERS
MAIN PROBLEM or EVENT

WHY? BECAUSE! MORE STORY KNOWLEDGE

GOAL

To improve story knowledge

BACKGROUND INFORMATION

The main focus of the *Why? Because!* lesson is to increase the students' overall story knowledge by helping them identify cause-and-effect relationships within a story. The students will be identifying, answering, and/or asking questions to discover cause-and-effect relationships. They will be aware that when asking about or explaining cause-and-effect relationships, they will use the key words *why* and *because*.

OBJECTIVES

1. Understand the concept of cause-and-effect relationships as used in a story context.
2. Recognize and use the key words *why* and *because* to signal cause-and-effect relationships.

MATERIALS

1. Einstein character (Recommended but not necessary; see page 12.)
2. A bag or container with treats (One treat per student)
3. *Why? Because!* graphic (See page 247; duplicate and enlarge the graphic, color it, mount it onto colorful construction paper or poster board, and laminate it for durability, if desired.)
4. *If You Give a Mouse a Cookie* (1985), by Laura Joffe Numeroff, illustrated by Felicia Bond (This book was chosen because it clearly illustrates what can happen [the effect] when you give a mouse a cookie [the cause]. This story also allows the students to use their predicting skills to guess what they think might happen next. Any story that clearly represents a cause-and-effect relationship can be used.)
5. *Why and Because Picture Cards* (See pages 248–250; duplicate them, color them, cut them apart, and laminate them for durability, if desired.)
6. *Why Questions* (See page 251.)

INTRODUCTION

Tie-in to Prior Learning

Einstein can remind the students that in the last lesson, they learned to tell what a story was mostly about rather that "clucking out the whole story." He can ask the students to use their whisper voices to tell what the story *Alexander and the Terrible, Horrible, No Good, Very Bad Day* is mostly about. If necessary, remind the students to tell only the main character(s) and main problem or event. Next, have Einstein ask why Alexander had such a bad day, and let a few students share some of the events that caused Alexander's bad day. Einstein can then ask:

> *What if Alexander had found a special prize in his cereal box, or his teacher had put his picture on the board with a big smiley face on top, or his mom had packed his favorite dessert in his lunchbox? Do you think the main event in our story might change?*

Have the students give the thumbs-up signal if they agree that Alexander's day might have changed from terrible to terrific. Ask the students why Alexander's day improved. Einstein can tell the class that he noticed that when he asked a *why* question, the students gave a *because* answer. (Write these two words on the board.) Tell the students that in today's lesson, they will be learning more about the concepts of why and because.

Focus/Relevancy

1. Have Einstein tell the students:

   > *Professor Green brought a special container to our classroom, just like this one!* (Show the bag or container of treats.) *When all the frogs looked inside, they got big smiles on their faces, just like yours! Why do you think everyone was smiling?*

   Emphasize the word *because* as it is used in the students' responses.

2. Tell the students that they have just demonstrated a *why* and *because* relationship.

   Ask the students why they were smiling when you held up the bag or container of treats. Below the word *why* on the board, draw a smiley face. Under the word *because,* draw a picture of the treat.

   Give several simple examples of this relationship (e.g., "Why do we wear a coat in the winter?" "Why do we need to eat nutritious or healthful foods?"). Use simple pictures or words under the appropriate terms on the board, as demonstrated in the example with the smiley face and the treat. Show the *Why? Because!* poster and talk about its meaning.

3. Relate the *why* and *because* relationship to problem solving by asking if the students have ever gone into a room and found a toy broken or something spilled on the floor and wondered how these events could have happened. Explain that when they discovered why such things happened, they should have learned to keep their toys away from a baby brother or sister, or not to leave a glass of milk too close to the edge of a table, for instance.

4. Einstein can tell the students they will be improving their story knowledge by discovering the *why* (the effect) and *because* (the cause) parts of a story:

   Just like we can tell why Alexander's day is terrible or terrific because of the bad events or good events in his day, I know that you are smiling because of this special bag (or container) *of treats.*

   You may choose to give each student a treat at this time or save them for the end of the lesson.

LESSON ACTIVITIES

1. Before reading the story *If You Give a Mouse a Cookie,* show the cover of the book, and let students predict what might happen if you give a mouse a cookie. Make a list of some of the students' ideas on the board. Then read the story.

2. Tell the students that because the mouse wanted a cookie, many things happened in our story. Explain that they will be helping match some of the *why* and *because* events from the story using the *Why and Because Picture Cards.* Explain to the students that they will be asked to come to the board and will be given a *why* picture from the story. Each *why* picture card has a sentence written on it. (The ten *because* pictures should be hung on the board in a column under the word *because.*) Each student will tell about his or her *why* picture (e.g., "The mouse wanted a straw"). Then the entire class will ask the *why* question, pertaining to the picture (e.g., "Why did the mouse want a straw?"). The student at the board may then choose a student to find the *because* picture from the pictures on the board and to tell the answer (e.g., "Because he wanted to drink his milk"). Continue to call on students until all the picture pairs have been chosen or until everyone has had a turn.

3. For additional practice, ask the *Why Questions*. Coach students to respond appropriately. Model the task for the students as needed.

CLOSURE

Summarize the lesson, repeat its relevance to students, and tie it to future learning. Einstein can congratulate the students on their ability to ask *why* questions and give *because* answers. They have been working hard to improve their story knowledge by learning the recipe for stories, how to put a story in order, how to tell what a story is mostly about, and, now, discovering the *why* and *because* in stories. Tell the students that in the next lesson, they will be reviewing everything that they have worked on in their language lessons.

Why?
Because!

Why and Because Picture Cards

The mouse asked for milk.

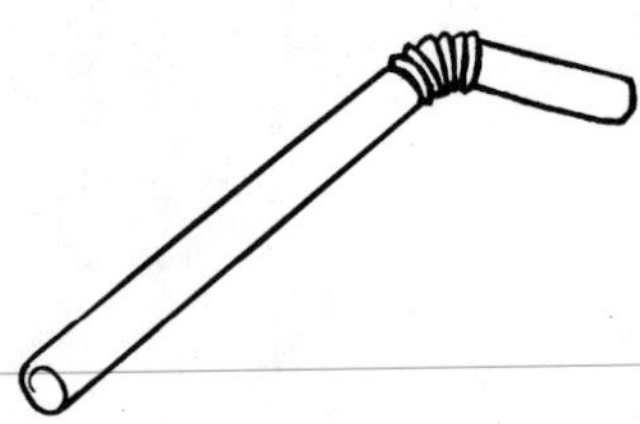

The mouse asked for a straw.

The mouse wanted to
look in the mirror.

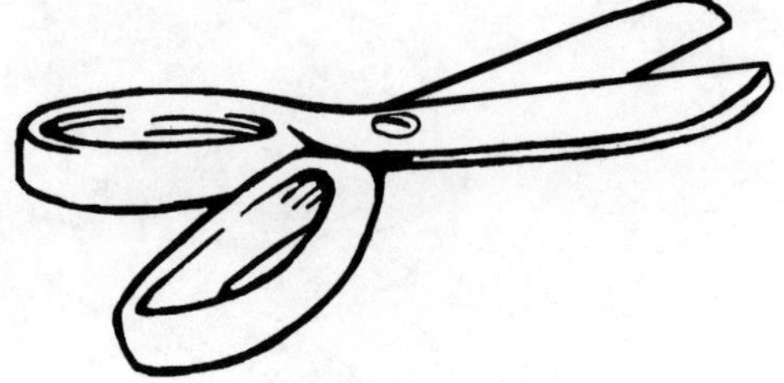

The mouse asked for
a pair of scissors.

The mouse wanted a broom.

The mouse wanted to take a nap.

The mouse asked for paper and crayons.

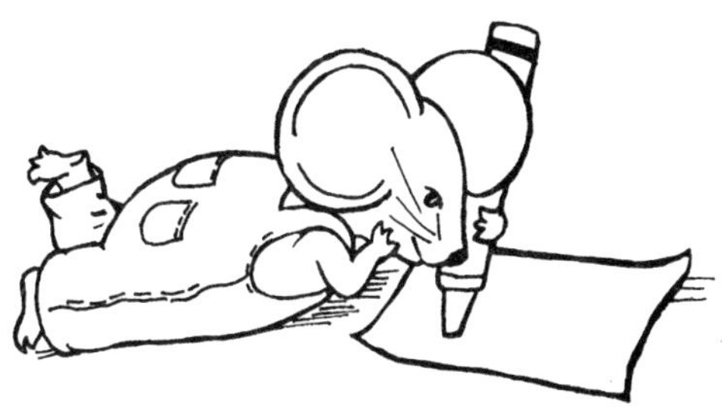

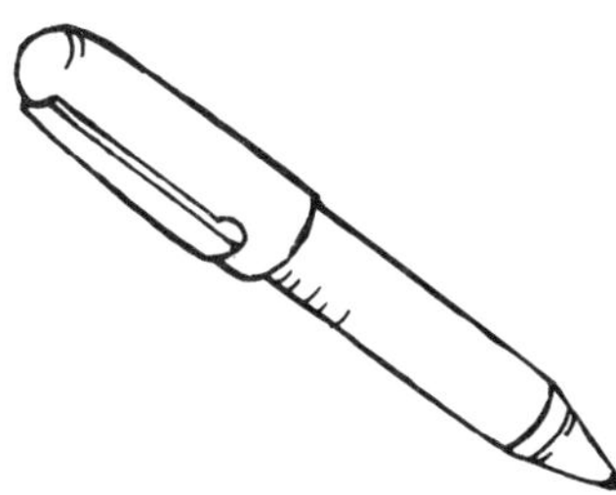

The mouse asked for a pen.

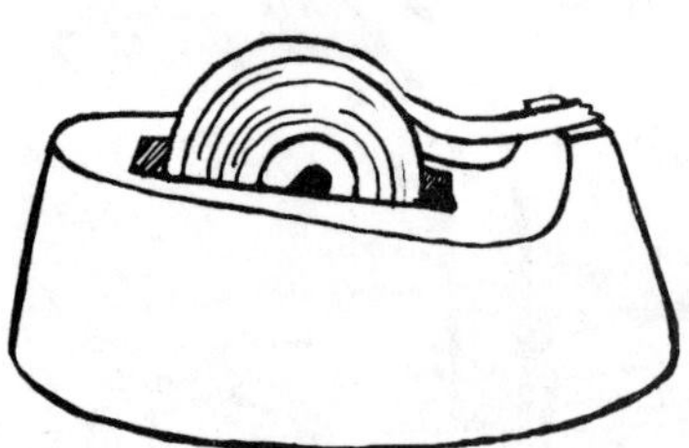

The mouse asked for the tape.

The mouse asked for a cookie.

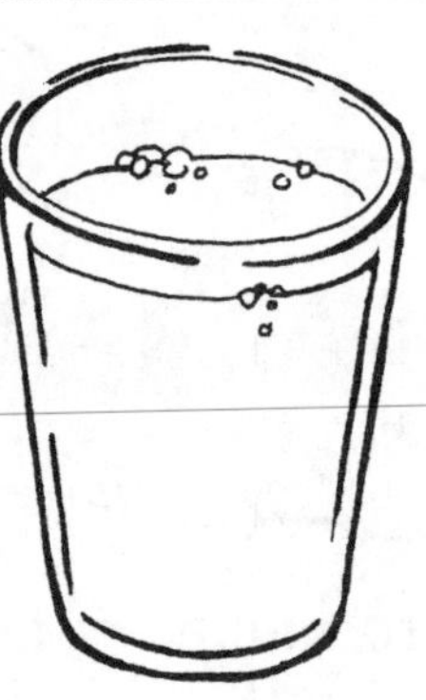

Why Questions

Why do we wear coats in the winter?

Why do we wear shoes?

Why do we water our plants?

Why do we brush our teeth?

Why do we look both ways before crossing the street?

Why do you go to school?

Why do we go to the doctor?

Why should you listen to your teachers?

Why do we wear a helmet when we ride our bike or Rollerblade?

Why might we need to use a flashlight or candles during a thunderstorm?

Why do we wash our hands before we eat?

Why do we turn on the air conditioner during the summer?

Why do we blow out candles on a cake?

Why would we carry an umbrella?

Why might someone give you a present?

STRATEGY REVIEW LESSON 5

GOAL

To reinforce and review the strategies for story knowledge

BACKGROUND INFORMATION

The main focus of this lesson is to review the story knowledge strategies: *Story Recipe, Follow the Detail Trail, Tell the Biggest Eggs, Why? Because!* A review lesson is provided after several strategies have been taught. In addition, the students take home *Homework Activity* pages and *Communication Skills Newsletter No. 5* to encourage parent involvement and understanding of the language skills.

OBJECTIVES

1. Review and practice the major components of the *Story Recipe, Follow the Detail Trail, Tell the Biggest Eggs,* and *Why? Because!* strategies.
2. Complete the application activities.
3. Share strategy information with family members.

MATERIALS

1. Einstein character (Recommended but not necessary; see page 12.)
2. *Story Recipe* poster (Created earlier)
3. *Follow the Detail Trail* poster (Created earlier)
4. *Tell the Biggest Eggs* poster (Created earlier)
5. *Why? Because!* poster (Created earlier)
6. *Homework Activity* pages (See pages 254–257; duplicate for each student.)
7. *Skills Checklist* (See page 258; duplicate and enlarge the checklist, color it, mount it onto colorful construction paper or poster board, and laminate it, if desired.)
8. *Communication Skills Newsletter No. 5* (See page 259–260; duplicate for each student.)

INTRODUCTION

Tie-in to Prior Learning

Have Einstein remind the students they have been learning many important skills to help them develop story knowledge. Display and briefly review the posters and strategies for these lessons.

Focus/Relevancy

Einstein can remind the students about the last time they had homework, and he can compliment the students on what a good job they did teaching their families about word power. He can tell them that they are going to have another special homework assignment, to be worked on with an older family member. Tell the students that their families will be really impressed when they hear how much they have learned!

LESSON ACTIVITIES

1. Briefly show the students the *Homework Activity* pages, and relate the questions on the sheets to the posters (*Story Recipe, Follow the Detail Trail, Tell the Biggest Eggs,* and *Why? Because!*) on the board.
2. Have Einstein select several students to model answers for the class, or have the entire class give choral responses to review questions from the *Homework Activity* pages.
3. Display the *Skills Checklist*. Review the key components of a lesson while looking at the poster and by practicing some items from the *Homework Activity* pages. Place or have students place a checkmark on the line beside each skill as the review is completed.
4. Show the students *Communication Skills Newsletter No. 5*. Explain that even their parents have homework. The newsletter describes the activities that they have been doing in class.
5. Hand out the *Homework Activity* pages and *Communication Skills Newsletter No. 5* for the students to take home, or place them in envelopes for students to take home.

CLOSURE

Summarize the lesson, repeat its relevance to students, and tie it to future learning. Have Einstein encourage the students to share their *Homework Activity* pages and *Communication Skills Newsletter No. 5* with someone special at home. Explain that after they have completed the homework, they should have their parent or caregiver sign and date in the appropriate space and return it for a reward (e.g., a sticker or points on a homework chart). Have Einstein congratulate the students on their use of story knowledge strategies. They can identify the ingredients of a good story, use sequence words to organize their ideas clearly, tell what a story is mostly about, and identify the causes of different events in a story. Tell the students that in the next lesson, they will be playing a game using all the strategies and skills they have learned this year.

Homework Activity

Name: ____________________

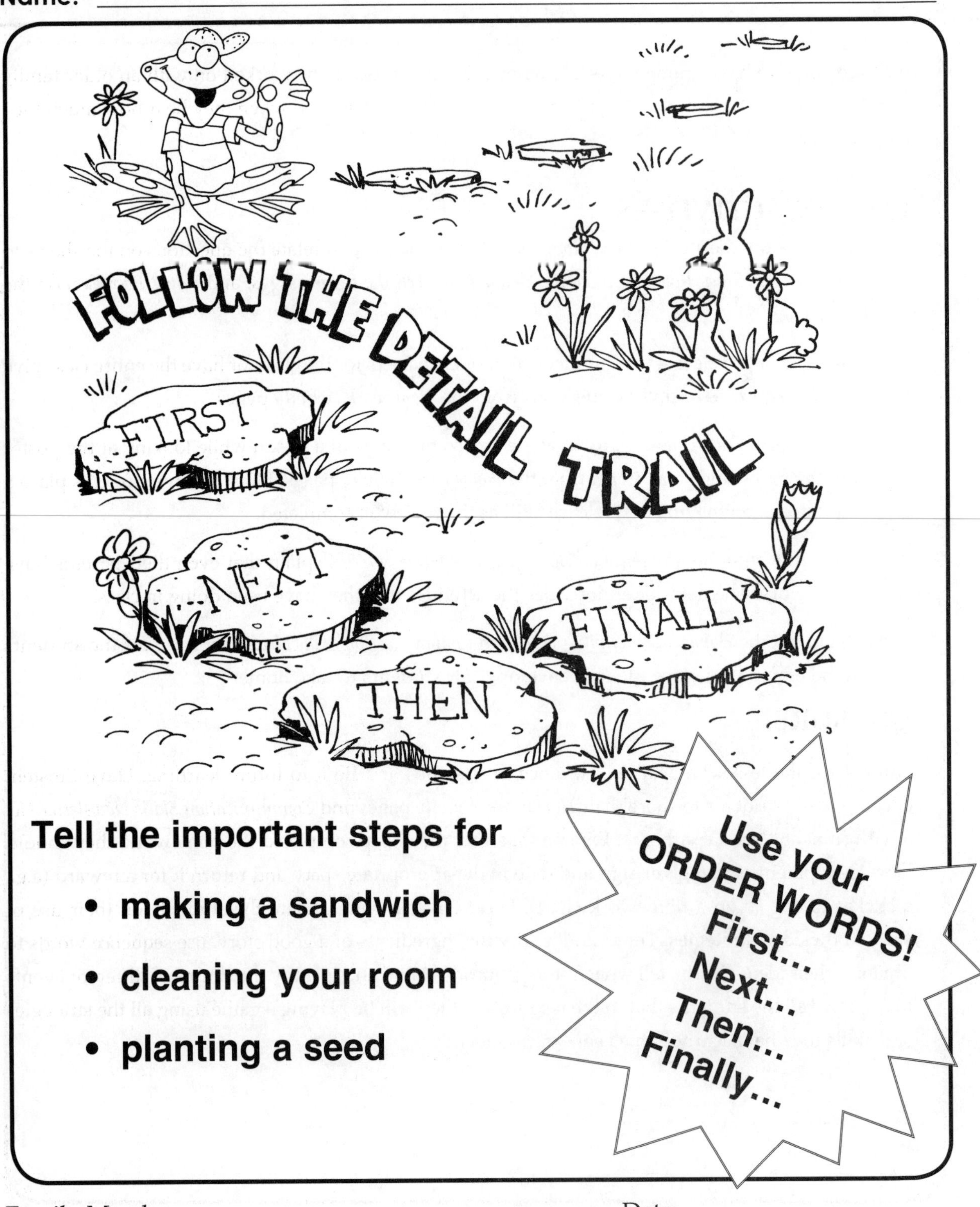

Family Member: ____________________ Date: ____________________

Homework Activity

Name: ______________________________

Sequence the pictures...
Use your ORDER WORDS!

First...	Next...	Then...	Finally...

cut along dotted lines

summer	spring	winter	fall

Family Member: ______________________ Date: ______________

Homework Activity

Name: ______________________________

Create your own story by drawing the ingredients! Mix up a good one!

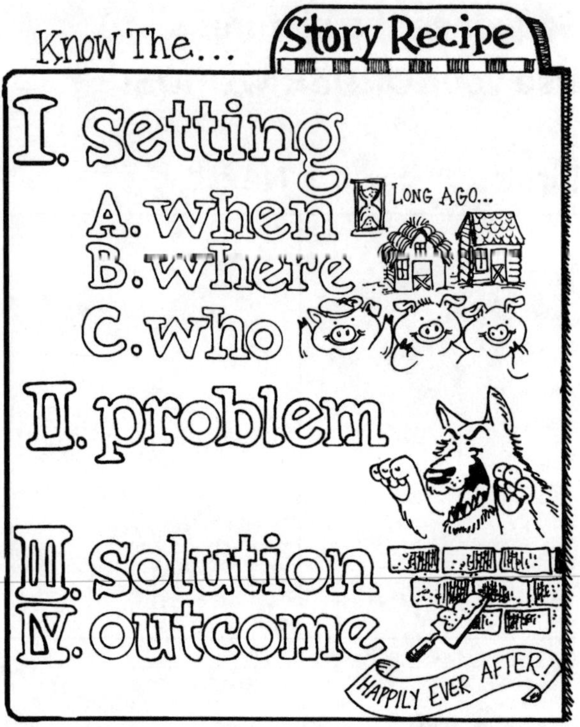

Know The... Story Recipe

I. setting
A. when — LONG AGO...
B. where
C. who
II. problem
III. solution
IV. outcome — HAPPILY EVER AFTER!

WHEN	WHERE	WHO
PROBLEM	SOLUTION	OUTCOME

Family Member: ______________________ Date: ____________

Homework Activity

Name: ____

Tell the main idea.
Don't cluck out the whole story!
Tell only the BIGGEST EGGS!

For each of the following tell:

the main character(s) (who) and

the main problem or event (what).

1. ***The Very Quiet Cricket***
2. ***Cinderella***
3. ***Alexander and the Terrible, Horrible, No Good, Very Bad Day***

Family Member: ______________________________ Date: ____________________

Skills Checklist

Skill ✓ Up

1. **I know the *ingredients* for telling a story: *When, Where, Who, Problem, Solution, Outcome.*** ______

2. **I can tell the *main idea* of a story by telling the *main character(s)* (who) and the *main problem or event* (what).** ______

3. **I can follow the detail trail by using special order words: *first, next, then,* and *finally.*** ______

4. **I can explain things that happen by asking *why* or telling the *because* answer.** ______

Communication Skills Newsletter

No. 5

Mixing Together a Good Story

We have been expanding our knowledge of stories. We have learned about the ingredients that every good story should have. We even had an opportunity to "mix" a special story that had a surprise ending. (Ask your child what happened when we added imagination [dry ice] to our watery story.)

Using Order Words in Stories

Einstein the frog, our language learning friend, challenged the students to become better listeners and thinkers by asking them to listen carefully to a story so that they could put it in order using special sequence words: *first, next, then,* and *finally*. We read *The Mitten*, by Jan Brett, and unscrambled mitten-shaped messages that retold the story when put in the right order. We also discovered that the order words could help us to tell the important steps for almost anything! We practiced using our order words while we told how to make popcorn, a sandwich, etc. (First you get out bread, peanut butter, jelly, and a knife. Then…). Model the steps needed to complete simple tasks at home, such as, making a bed or making Jell-o, and have your child tell the order using sequence words (e.g., *First* you smooth the sheet, *then* you pull up the blanket…).

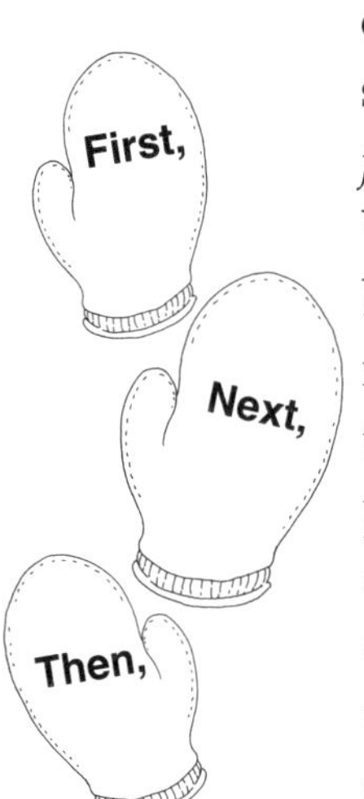

Our Story Recipe

Your child may want to make up stories about his or her adventures at home or on vacation. Our story recipe calls for a setting: When does the story take place (*long, long ago, on a stormy summer night,* or *last Saturday morning*)? Where does it happen (*in a forest, in a castle, at your house*)? Who is in the story (*the three pigs, a princess, your family*)? The next ingredient in the story recipe is the problem: *Is a big wolf chasing the characters?* or *Does the family dog keep escaping?* The problem needs a solution: *The wolf is captured* or *The fence is repaired to keep the dog in.* Finally, stories need an outcome: *The characters lived happily ever after* or *The children played with the dog every day, and he never ran away from home again.*

Summarizing a Story

An important school skill is the ability to summarize. Because we do not always need to tell the whole story, we learned to listen for what the story is mainly about. After listening to *Alexander and the Terrible, Horrible, No Good, Very Bad Day*, by Judith Viorst, we discovered that the details, which make the story fun, told us why Alexander had such a bad day, but they were not what the story was mainly about (e.g., Alexander got gum in his hair, had a cavity, and didn't get any dessert, which is why he had a bad day). After watching a video, cartoon, or reading a favorite story, have your child practice summarizing by telling the main characters and the main problem or event in the story.

Asking and Answering Hard Questions

We've been practicing how to answer more difficult questions about a story. The students learned about asking *why* questions and giving *because* answers. We read *If You Give a Mouse a Cookie*, by Laura Joffe Numeroff, which is full of cause/effect relationships. We practiced asking and answering questions about the story, such as, "Why did the mouse want a straw?" "Because he wanted to drink his milk." This skill requires the children to attend to the important details and how they are linked within the story.

Our Vacation Calendar

It is hard to believe that the vacation break is almost here again! Your child will be bringing home a vacation calendar of activities to reinforce language strategies that we have introduced during the year. These activities usually take less than five minutes per day to complete, but can provide a valuable reminder of important skills! Let's keep those brains in gear!

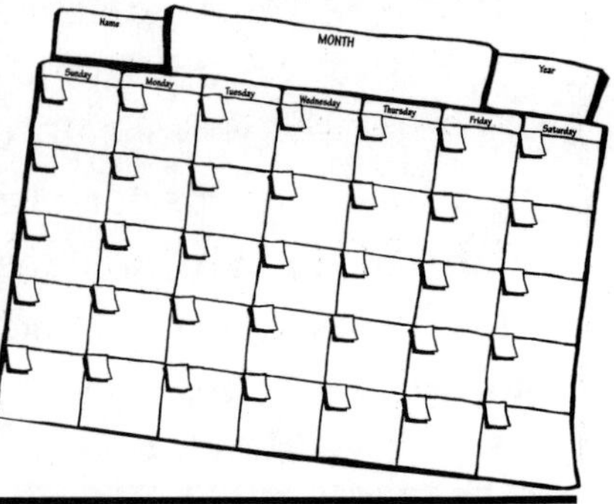

STRATEGY REVIEW VACATION CALENDAR

GOAL

To maintain strategy use

BACKGROUND INFORMATION

The main focus of this lesson is to provide a format for maintaining strategies during an extended break from school, in the form of a home review and practice calendar.

OBJECTIVES

1. Provide a method for review and practice of all language strategies to cover over an extended break from school.
2. Provide activities to encourage application of skills at home.

MATERIALS

1. Einstein character (Recommended but not necessary; see page 12.)
2. Posters for all strategies (Created earlier)
3. *Vacation Calendar* (See pages 263–264; add the year, months, and dates to the calendars. Then duplicate one per student.)

INTRODUCTION

Tie-in to Prior Learning

Einstein can remind the students that they have been improving their story knowledge so that they can be a part of the adventure by using their imagination, making predictions of what might happen next, and telling their own stories. They have also learned the ingredients that all good stories need, how to tell what the story is mostly about, and how to answer the *why* and *because* questions in a story.

Focus/Relevancy

Display all the strategy posters on the board while praising the students on their hard work this year. Have Einstein explain that he has a way for them to remember all the listening, word power, and story knowledge skills they have learned! Show the vacation calendar.

LESSON ACTIVITIES

1. Tell the students that the *Vacation Calendar* has quick, easy items to be practiced each day. Einstein is going to show them how it works by trying to "trick" them with some questions from this special calendar. Ask a variety of questions that review the different strategies.

Einstein can call on a student to come to the front of the room. Explain to the class that if the student needs help answering the question, or when choosing the next person to guess, he or she will only call on students who are sitting quietly and raising their hand.

2. After reviewing a number of strategy items from the calendar, reinforce the importance of sharing this information at home, along with the ease and fun of doing these assignments. Students can really impress their friends and family with what they have learned!

3. Stress that each activity takes only minutes to complete. Suggest hanging the calendar in a visible place (e.g., on the refrigerator) so that students and family members will not forget to do the activities. Tell the students that they can earn a special reward by returning the completed calendars, whose activities have been initialed by parents, after the vacation from school.

   Hand out the calendars directly to the students, or place them in an envelope to take home.

CLOSURE

Summarize the lesson, repeat its relevance to students, and tie it to future learning. Emphasize that by practicing the activities on the calendar, the students will be "ahead of the game" when they return to school.

Say to the students:

> *I hope that you all will be great listeners, powerful speakers, and have lots of story knowledge when you come back to school after the long vacation!*

Directions: Initial each activity when you've done it with your child. Save the calendar and send it back to school after vacation.

Name | MONTH | Year

Sunday	Monday	Tuesday	Wednesday	Thursday	Friday	Saturday
What sounds do you hear in your house? (Listen carefully!)	When I listen, my brain is working and my mouth is ________.	When I listen, my eyes are on the speaker and my body is ________.	When I listen, my hands are ________.	When I don't understand, I can… Request CLARIFICATION "Excuse me, but did you mean…?"	Listen for sounds in your backyard.	Go for a swim but don't forget your mittens! "Excuse me, but…?"
When I describe, I use my five ________.	Observe an ant. Tell two size words.	What shape is • a baseball? • a house? • a refrigerator?	What is a distinctive feature of a skunk?	What is your distinctive feature? What makes you special?	Give a color word for • the sky • grass • the pool	Tell how each of these smell and taste: • lemon • chips • candy
Have a big, bright, sticky, ice-cold, sweet sno-cone!	List four pets. (How many can you think of for this group?)	What category do these fit into? • cookies • cakes • pies	Airplanes, hot air balloons, and kites are all ________.	Name things that melt.	Name green things.	Play something from the "sports" group!
Observe things that are *alike* and *different*.	*Comparing* tells how things are the same or ________.	*Contrasting* tells how things are ________.	Compare and contrast a swimming pool and a lake (give one "alike" and one "different").	Compare and contrast a tiger and a bumble bee (give one "alike" and one "different").	Would you choose bubblegum or a candy bar? Why?	Do a cartwheel!
Read a good book!	Name a word that rhymes with *each* and *peach*. ________	Can you discover the pattern? • big • pig • dig	Tell two words that rhyme with *hop*. ______ ______	When I observe, I use my ________.	Describe how the sidewalk feels on your bare feet on a hot summer day.	Use your sequence words to tell how to make your favorite snack.

Directions: Initial each activity when you've done it with your child. Save the calendar and send it back to school after vacation.

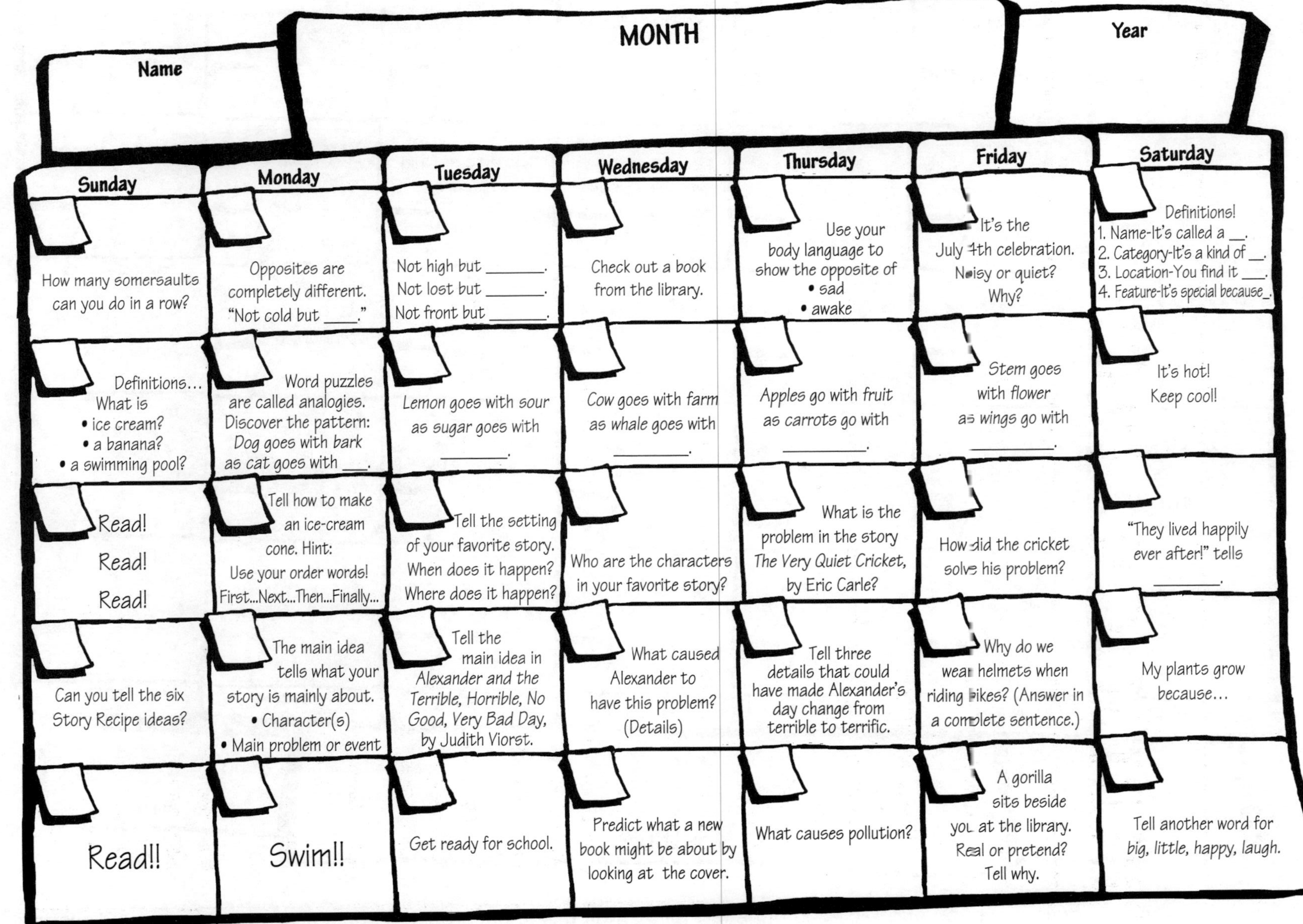

Name | MONTH | Year

Sunday	Monday	Tuesday	Wednesday	Thursday	Friday	Saturday
How many somersaults can you do in a row?	Opposites are completely different. "Not cold but ____."	Not high but ______. Not lost but ______. Not front but ______.	Check out a book from the library.	Use your body language to show the opposite of • sad • awake	It's the July 4th celebration. Noisy or quiet? Why?	Definitions! 1. Name-It's called a __. 2. Category-It's a kind of __. 3. Location-You find it __. 4. Feature-It's special because_.
Definitions… What is • ice cream? • a banana? • a swimming pool?	Word puzzles are called analogies. Discover the pattern: *Dog goes with bark as cat goes with* ___.	*Lemon goes with sour as sugar goes with* ______.	*Cow goes with farm as whale goes with* ______.	*Apples go with fruit as carrots go with* ______.	*Stem goes with flower as wings go with* ______.	It's hot! Keep cool!
Read! Read! Read!	Tell how to make an ice-cream cone. Hint: Use your order words! First...Next...Then...Finally...	Tell the setting of your favorite story. When does it happen? Where does it happen?	Who are the characters in your favorite story?	What is the problem in the story *The Very Quiet Cricket*, by Eric Carle?	How did the cricket solve his problem?	"They lived happily ever after!" tells ______.
Can you tell the six Story Recipe ideas?	The main idea tells what your story is mainly about. • Character(s) • Main problem or event	Tell the main idea in *Alexander and the Terrible, Horrible, No Good, Very Bad Day*, by Judith Viorst.	What caused Alexander to have this problem? (Details)	Tell three details that could have made Alexander's day change from terrible to terrific.	Why do we wear helmets when riding bikes? (Answer in a complete sentence.)	My plants grow because…
Read!!	Swim!!	Get ready for school.	Predict what a new book might be about by looking at the cover.	What causes pollution?	A gorilla sits beside you at the library. Real or pretend? Tell why.	Tell another word for *big, little, happy, laugh.*

BIBLIOGRAPHY

Alexander and the Terrible, Horrible, No Good, Very Bad Day (1972)
by Judith Viorst, illustrated by Ray Cruz
New York: Atheneum
ISBN 0-689-30072-7

Caps, Hats, Socks, and Mittens: A Book about the Four Seasons (1992)
by Louise Borden, illustrated by Lillian Hoban
New York: Scholastic
ISBN 0-590-44872-2

Dinner at the Panda Palace (1995), by Stephanie Calmenson, illustrated by Nadine Bernard Westcott
New York: HarperTrophy
ISBN 0-06-443408-7

Each Peach Pear Plum (1979), by Janet and Allan Ahlberg
New York: Puffin Books
ISBN 0-14-050639-X

The Happy Hedgehog Band (1992), by Martin Waddell, illustrated by Jill Barton
Cambridge, MA: Candlewick Press
ISBN 1-56402-011-8

If You Give a Mouse a Cookie (1985), by Laura Joffe Numeroff, illustrated by Felicia Bond
New York: HarperCollins
ISBN 0-06-024586-7

Is Your Mama a Llama? (1989), by Deborah Guarino, illustrated by Steven Kellogg
New York: Scholastic
ISBN 0-590-41387-2

Let's Go Home, Little Bear (1993), by Martin Waddell, illustrated by Barbara Firth
Cambridge MA: Candlewick Press
ISBN 1-56402-131-9

Listen to the Rain (1988), by Bill Martin Jr. and John Archambault, illustrated by James Endicott
New York: Holt
ISBN 0-8050-0682-6

The Mitten: A Ukranian Folktale (1989), adapted by Jan Brett
New York: G.P. Putnam's Sons
ISBN 0 399 21920 X

Mufaro's Beautiful Daughters: An African Tale (1987), by John L. Steptoe, translated by Clarita Kohen
New York: Lothrop
ISBN 0-688-04045-4

The Paper Bag Princess (1980), by Robert N. Munsch, illustrated by Michael Martchenko
Toronto: Annick Press
ISBN 0-920236-16-2

Possum Magic (1991), by Mem Fox, illustrated by Julie Vivas
San Diego: Harcourt Brace Jovanovich
ISBN 0-15-263224-7

The Princess and the Pea (1979), by Hans Christian Andersen, illustrated by Paul Galdone
New York: Houghton Mifflin
ISBN 0-395-28807-X

Rocking Horse Christmas (1997), by Mary Pope Osborne, illustrated by Ned Bittinger
New York: Scholastic
ISBN 0-590-92955-0

Sheep Out to Eat (1995), by Nancy Shaw, illustrated by Margot Apple
Boston: Houghton Mifflin
ISBN 0-395-72027-3

That's Good! That's Bad! (1993), by Margery Cuyler, illustrated by David Catrow
Madison, WI: Demco Media
ISBN 0-606-06054-5

The Three Little Javelinas (1992), by Susan Lowell, illustrated by Jim Harris
Flagstaff, AZ: Northland
ISBN 0-87358-542-9

Too Much Noise (1992), by Ann McGovern, illustrated by Simms Taback
Boston: Houghton Mifflin
ISBN 0-395-62985-3

The Very Quiet Cricket: A Multi-Sensory Book (1990), by Eric Carle
New York: Philomel Books
ISBN 0-399-21885-8

Who Is the Beast? (1990), by Keith Baker
San Diego, CA: Harcourt Brace
ISBN 0-15-296057-0

REFERENCES

Baker, K. (1990). *Who is the beast?* San Diego, CA: Harcourt Brace.

Bloom, B.S. (1956). *Taxonomy of educational objectives.* New York: Longman.

Caine, R., and Caine, G. (1991). *Making connections teaching and the human brain.* Menlo Park, CA: Innovative Learning Publications.

Genishi, C. (1988). *Young children's oral language development.* ERIC Clearinghouse on Elementary and Early Childhood Education, Urbana, IL. (ERIC Document Reproduction Service No. ED 301 361)

Hunter, M. (1982). *Mastery teaching.* El Segundo, CA: TIP Publications.

Jalongo, M. (1991). *Strategies for developing children's listening skills.* (Fastback No. 314). (Available from the Phi Delta Kappa Educational Foundation, P.O. Box 789, Bloomington, IN 47402)

Johnson, D., Johnson, R., and Johnson Holubec, E. (1990). *Circles of learning* (3rd ed.), Edina, MN: Interaction Book.

Kagan, S. (1994). *Cooperative learning.* San Clemente, CA: Kagan Cooperative Learning.

Kavalic, S., and Olsen, K. (1993). *ITI: The model-integrated thematic instruction.* Village of Oak Creek, AZ: Kavalik.

McInroy, J. (1996, February). *I told him 100 times!* Presentation at in-service for speech-language pathologists at the Education Service Center, Region X, Richardson, TX.

Naremore, R. (1995). *Language intervention with school-aged children: Conversation, narrative, and text.* San Diego, CA: Singular.

Oxford, R. (1994). *Language learning strategies: An update.* ERIC Digest. ERIC Clearinghouse on Languages and Linguistics, Washington, DC. (ERIC Document Reproduction Service No. ED 376 707)

Rief, S.F. (1993). *How to reach and teach ADD/ADHD children.* West Nyack, NY: The Center for Applied Research in Education.

Wagner, B. (1989). *Whole language: Integrating the language arts—and much more.* The ERIC Digest. ERIC Clearinghouse on Reading and Communication Skills, Bloomington, IN. (ERIC Document Reproduction Service No. ED 313 675)